Peter Albrecht, Paul Jackson (Eds)

Security Sector Reform in Sierra Leone 1997 – 2007: Views from the Front Line

AF721825

Geneva Centre for the
Democratic Control of Armed Forces
(DCAF)

LIT

Security Sector Reform in Sierra Leone 1997 – 2007: Views from the Front Line

edited by

Peter Albrecht and Paul Jackson

LIT

∞

Gedruckt auf alterungsbeständigem Werkdruckpapier entsprechend
ANSI Z3948 DIN ISO 9706

Bibliographic information published by the Deutsche Nationalbibliothek
The Deutsche Nationalbibliothek lists this publication in the Deutsche Nationalbibliografie; detailed bibliographic data are available in the Internet at http://dnb.d-nb.de.

ISBN 978-3-643-80063-3

A catalogue record for this book is available from the British Library

©LIT VERLAG Dr. W. Hopf Berlin 2010
Fresnostr. 2 D-48159 Münster
Tel. +49 (0) 2 51-620 320 Fax +49 (0) 2 51-922 60 99
e-Mail: lit@lit-verlag.de http://www.lit-verlag.de

Distribution:
In Germany: LIT Verlag Fresnostr. 2, D-48159 Münster
Tel. +49 (0) 2 51-620 32 22, Fax +49 (0) 2 51-922 60 99, e-Mail: vertrieb@lit-verlag.de

In Austria: Medienlogistik Pichler-ÖBZ, e-mail: mlo@medien-logistik.at

In Switzerland: B + M Buch- und Medienvertrieb, e-mail: order@buch-medien.ch

In the UK: Global Book Marketing, e-mail: mo@centralbooks.com

In North America by:

Transaction Publishers
New Brunswick (U.S.A.) and London (U.K.)

Transaction Publishers
Rutgers University
35 Berrue Circle
Piscataway, NJ 08854

Phone: +1 (732) 445 - 2280
Fax: + 1 (732) 445 - 3138
for orders (U. S. only):
toll free (888) 999 - 6778
e-mail: orders@transactionpub.com

Contents

Part III: Sierra Leone Perspectives

Part IV: Conclusion

Preface

Sierra Leone is often cited as *the* example of effective and sustainable security sector reform (SSR). In particular, the SSR process is characterised as an effective partnership between national stakeholders and the international community, notably the United Kingdom. However, this picture lacks the nuance and contextual detail necessary to deconstruct the SSR process in Sierra Leone and derive meaningful lessons learned. This publication will go a long way in adding subtlety and detail to our understanding of this important case.

The work of the Geneva Centre for the Democratic Control of Armed Forces (DCAF) places a strong premium on policy research grounded in concrete experience. This reflects the need to bridge evident gaps between SSR policy and practice through analysis that is closely linked to context-specific political, security and socio-economic factors. We are therefore delighted to support this goal through the publication of *Security Sector Reform in Sierra Leone 1997-2007: Views from the Front Line*.

A core value that underpins DCAF's policy and operational work is commitment to the principle of local ownership. The concept of local ownership is a challenging one, increasingly criticised as a ubiquitous and anodyne policy prescription rarely operationalised in practice.[1] This volume is particularly valuable in moving forward the discussion on this issue. Sierra Leoneans and their UK counterparts who have all participated in this process provide analysis of the design and implementation of SSR over a ten-year period. This helps clarify the challenges, tensions and problem-solving approaches that evolved over time as part of this process. DCAF therefore hopes that disseminating and discussing the findings contained in this volume in different forums will provide insights that can make a concrete impact on the design, implementation and effectiveness of SSR policies and programming.

It would not have been possible to complete this volume successfully without the invaluable support of a number of people. In particular, I would

---

1 DCAF's 2008 Year Book addresses issues of local ownership and SSR from both thematic and different geographical perspectives. See Donais, T. (ed.) *Local Ownership and Security Sector Reform* (Munster: Lit Verlag, 2008). Also available online at: www.dcaf.ch/publications.

like to acknowledge the commitment and skill of the editors, Paul Jackson and Peter Albrecht, in refining a great deal of experience and expertise from a range of different actors into the nuanced analysis found within this volume. Fairlie Chappuis provided important research assistance during the editing process, while DCAF colleague Jonathan Sandy gave generously of his time and unparalleled expertise in providing incisive comments and inputs on earlier drafts of the manuscript. In particular, thanks go to the chapter contributors; this work is important exactly because it provides such a frank and open analysis of individual and collective experience of the security sector reform process in Sierra Leone.[2]

Alan Bryden
Deputy Head of Research
DCAF

Geneva, May 2010

---

2 The views expressed in this volume are those of the authors alone and do not in any way represent the views of the institutions or their representatives involved in this project.

List of Abbreviations

ACC	Anti-Corruption Commission
ACPP	Africa Conflict Prevention Pool
AFRC	Armed Forces Revolutionary Council
AFRICOM	Africa Command
APC	All People's Congress
AU	African Union
BPRM	Bo Peace and Reconciliation Movement
CCSSP	Commonwealth Community Safety and Security Project
CDF	Civil Defence Force
CDIID	Complaints, Discipline and Internal Investigation Department
CID	Criminal Investigation Department
CIMIC	civil-military cooperation
CISU	Central Intelligence and Security Unit
CIVPOL	UN Civilian Police Force
CR	Conciliation Resources
CSSP	Commonwealth Safety and Security Programme
DACO	Development Assistance Coordination Office
DDR	disarmament, demobilisation and reintegration
DFID	UK Department for International Development
DISEC	district security committee
ECOMOG	ECOWAS Monitoring Group
ECOWAS	Economic Community of West African States
EUCOM	European Command
FCO	UK Foreign and Commonwealth Office
FSU	Family Support Unit
GCSRP	Governance and Civil Service Reform Programme
GoSL	government of Sierra Leone
HQ	headquarters
HRMO	human resource management office
IGP	inspector-general of police
IMATT	International Military Assistance Training Team
ISA	intelligence and security adviser
ISS	intelligence and security service
JAT	joint assessment team

JFC	joint force commander
JIC	Joint Intelligence Committee
JMA	joint maritime authority
JSC	joint support command(er)
JSDP	Justice Sector Development Programme
JSRS	justice sector reform strategy
KAIDCSO	Kailahun District Civil Society Organisations
KIA	killed in action
LAN	local area network
LNP	Liberia National Police
LNP	local needs policing
LPPB	local policing partnership board
MACP	military aid to civil power
MDAs	ministries, departments and agencies
MIA	Ministry of Internal Affairs
MIB	Military Intelligence Branch
MoD	Ministry of Defence
MODAT	Ministry of Defence Assistance Team
MoF	Ministry of Finance
MoU	memorandum of understanding
NEC	National Election Commission
NEPAD	New Partnership for Africa's Development
NGO	non-governmental organisation
NPRC	National Provisional Ruling Council
NSA	national security architecture
NSC	National Security Council
NSCCG	National Security Council Coordinating Group
NSSR	national security sector review
ODA	UK Overseas Development Administration
OECD DAC	Development Assistance Committee of the Organisation for Economic Co-operation and Development
OGD	other government department
ONS	Office of National Security
OSD	Operational Support Division
POCDI&PA	Parliamentary Oversight Committee on Defence, Internal and Presidential Affairs
PROSEC	provincial security committee
PRSP	poverty reduction strategy paper
PSO	peace support operations
RSLAF	Republic of Sierra Leone Armed Forces

RSLMF	Republic of Sierra Leone Military Force
RUF	Revolutionary United Front
SB	Special Branch
SES	senior executive service
SILSEP	Sierra Leone Security Sector Programme
SLA	Sierra Leone Army
SLP	Sierra Leone Police
SLPP	Sierra Leone People's Party
SSER	security sector expenditure review
SSR	security sector reform
UK	United Kingdom
UN	United Nations
UNAMSIL	UN Mission in Sierra Leone
UNDP	UN Development Programme
UNICEF	UN Children's Fund
UNIOSIL	UN Integrated Office in Sierra Leone
WAN	wide area network
WG	working group
WIA	wounded in action

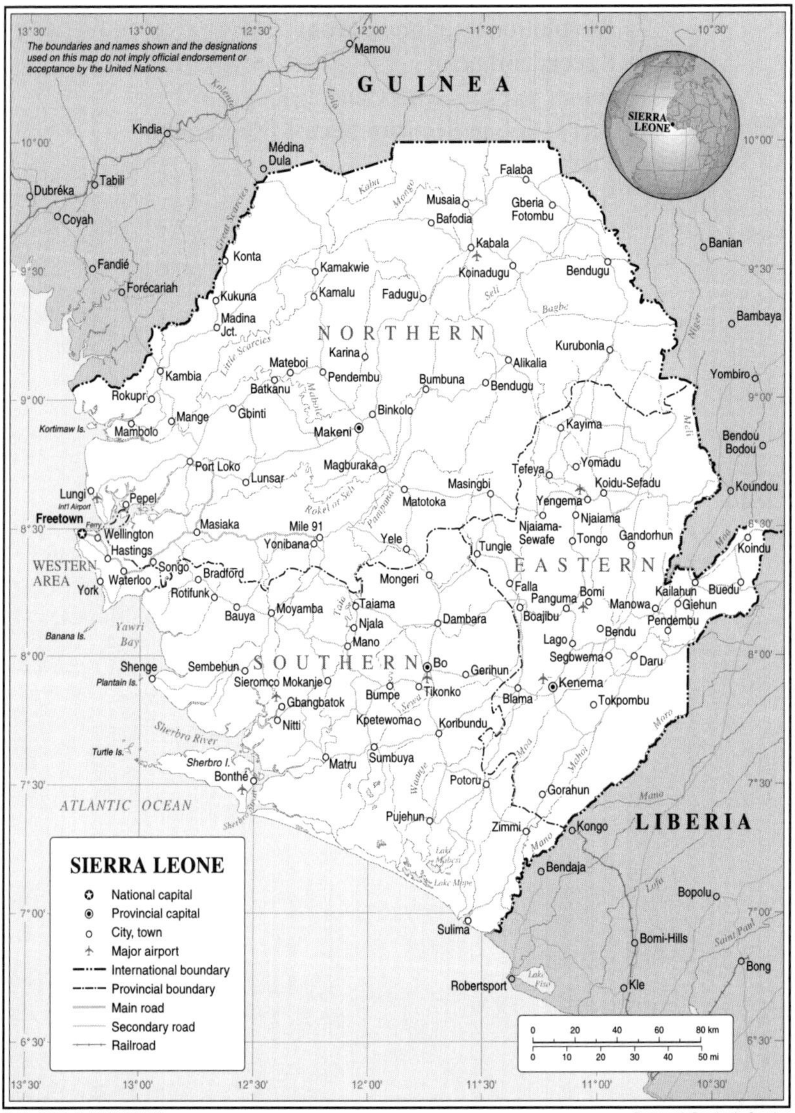

Map No. 3902 Rev. 5 UNITED NATIONS
January 2004

Department for Peacekeeping Operations
Cartographic Section

Part I

Introduction

Chapter 1

Introduction: The Roots of Security Sector Reform in Sierra Leone

Paul Jackson and Peter Albrecht

This book represents an attempt to bring together some of the diverse voices within the Sierra Leonean security sector reform (SSR) experience between 1997 and 2007. Within this period there was substantial international intervention by the United Nations and also by the United Kingdom, and a huge post-war intervention led by the UK and designed to reconstruct completely a state that had effectively ceased to exist. A key element of this reconstruction was the redesign of the security system, and this volume aims to bring together a number of those who were directly involved in that process.

As a collection of separate papers, this volume is not aimed at being a coherent, polished version of the security transformation of Sierra Leone, but at providing an insight into the thoughts of those involved. In particular we have sought to showcase papers providing a 'warts-and-all' picture of the reform process that not everyone would agree with, but all have to acknowledge as being relevant. The original idea of these papers was to provide inputs into a broader piece of research reconstructing the narrative of the UK intervention, so many of them were not written with publication in mind. Rather, the authors sought to provide their own views of the process from their particular vantage point and to highlight different perceptions of the same processes.

By the end of the war in 2002 there was, in fact, very little of any state left to reconstruct. In the countryside the Revolutionary United Front (RUF) had targeted firstly the paramount chiefs and then any representative of the central government. This included civil servants, local government officers, buildings and records. By 2002 there were very few government records remaining and most officials had fled, particularly from the countryside. The Sierra Leonean state had effectively ceased to exist. The group that is represented here in this volume, therefore, inherited an almost blank slate in terms of reforms.

In 2007, for the first time in two decades, Sierra Leone conducted a generally peaceful national election without international peacekeeping assistance. These elections were conducted *by* and *for* the people of Sierra Leone, who exercised their right to vote in a generally orderly environment made possible by their own security forces, which had been completely reformed, trained and armed.

Seen within the context of the levels of violence experienced by the people of Sierra Leone in the previous 20 years, the fact that Sierra Leone conducted this generally violence-free election only seven years after the end of a civil war is a remarkable transformation. This transformation is due to improved personal security that resulted from substantial UN and UK intervention and assistance, but also the leadership of a core of Sierra Leonean government officials who have sustained the security reform effort over an extended period of time, often in difficult circumstances. This volume brings together some of the thoughts of those officials on the processes in which they were engaged.

The Context of Sierra Leone

In many ways Sierra Leone is a small and insignificant country on the west coast of Africa. In the bottom few countries in the UN Development Programme's (UNDP) Human Development Index, until the 2009 index Sierra Leone ranked 177 out of 177 countries. In 2009 this improved to 180 out of 182, above only Niger and Afghanistan.[1] While purchasing power parity GDP per capita is around $679, life expectancy is only 47.3 years and there is just a 30 per cent probability of living until 40 years old. The adult illiteracy rate is over 60 per cent and the female literacy rate is half the male. By almost any measure Sierra Leone remains a very poor country, which rather begs questions regarding the 'success' of the external intervention.

However, given the levels of violence experienced during a protracted war and also the nature of that war itself, Sierra Leone must be seen as a success. The vast majority of the population now live without the fear of extreme violence that haunted the country for at least ten years during the war, and before that inside a rapacious and authoritarian state. In 1994 Robert Kaplan identified Sierra Leone as a key area of study since it was representative of the 'coming anarchy' of collapsing states.[2] In Kaplan's analysis the world was divided into a small group of very rich countries and chaos. Sierra Leone represented the chaos: a mixture of demographic, environmental and social factors epitomised by gangs of rootless youth with no social ties to control them.

Kaplan used Sierra Leone to introduce his extremely influential article by saying:

> Sierra Leone is a microcosm of what is occurring, albeit in a more tempered and gradual manner, throughout West Africa and much of the underdeveloped world: the withering away of central governments, the rise of tribal and regional domains, the unchecked spread of disease, and the growing pervasiveness of war. West Africa is reverting to the Africa of the Victorian Atlas. It consists now of a series of coastal trading posts, such as Freetown and Conakry, and an interior that, owing to violence, volatility and disease, is again becoming, as Graham Greene once observed, 'blank' and 'unexplored'. However, whereas Greene's vision implies a certain romance, as in the somnolent and charmingly seedy Freetown of his celebrated novel *The Heart of the Matter*, it is Thomas Malthus, the philosopher of demographic doomsday, who is now the prophet of West Africa's future. And West Africa's future, eventually, will also be that of most of the rest of the world.[3]

Despite his lack of knowledge of African political history, Kaplan's thesis is basically that the modern state is dying and Africans are reverting to 'traditional' forms of organisation that are not constrained by modern laws and human rights – and Sierra Leone was an archetype of this development. Unsurprisingly perhaps, this thesis has been subject to withering criticism from those who worked in and on Sierra Leone.[4] Despite this, Kaplan's analysis did have some resonance with several policy-makers dealing with the aftermath of the Cold War and the end of a bipolar world.

While Kaplan's analysis is clearly problematic, it managed to get Sierra Leone on to the agendas of several Western countries, particularly in the UK. In many ways, Sierra Leone seemed to represent a microcosm of all that was falling apart in the post-Cold War world, particularly in Africa. Warlords, shadow economies, collapsing states and the ensuing violence were all present in Sierra Leone, along with environmental degradation, illegal trading, child soldiers and extreme violence against civilians. Certainly, within the UK it became a country that could not be allowed to disappear, since if the international community could not save Sierra Leone then where could it save?

Along with the violence, Sierra Leone is probably best known for diamonds. The alluvial diamonds that should have made the country rich have given the world the phenomenon of 'blood diamonds' or 'conflict diamonds'. While analysts such as Richards and Keen[5] point out that attributing the war to diamonds is a gross oversimplification, the alluvial diamond fields certainly did play a role in prolonging the conflict and motivating some of the leaders of both sides.[6] At the same time, the diamonds played a role in terms of encouraging some leaders to continue violence in order to mine the rich seam of diamond trading, and also acting as a magnet for various forms of private sector intervention in the country. In fact, still today, diamond mining, corruption and smuggling remain important governance issues within Sierra Leone and across the Mano River region more broadly.

Lastly, the war became internationally famous for the brutality shown towards civilians, with around 70,000 estimated as casualties and around half the population of 5 million people being internally displaced or fleeing into Guinea or Liberia. The deliberate targeting of civilians became a characteristic of a war that left many traumatised either mentally or through the physical removal of limbs. A frequently cited Human Right Watch report explains the approach adopted by the rebels on entering Freetown in 1999:

> The rebel occupation of Freetown was characterized by the systematic and widespread perpetration of all classes of gross human rights abuses against the civilian population. Civilians were gunned down within their houses, rounded up and massacred on the streets, thrown from the upper floors of buildings, used as human shields, and burnt alive in cars and houses. They had their limbs hacked off with machetes, eyes gouged out with knives, hands smashed with hammers, and bodies burned with boiling water. Women and girls were systematically sexually abused, and children and young people abducted by the hundreds. The rebels made little distinction between civilian and military targets. They repeatedly stated that they believed civilians should be punished for what they perceived to be their support for the existing government. Thus the rebels waged war against the civilian population through their perpetration of human rights abuses. While there was some targeting of particular groups, such as Nigerians, police officers, journalists and church workers, the vast majority of atrocities were committed by rebels who chose their victims apparently at random…
>
> …The atrocities were often planned and premeditated. Victims and witnesses describe well-organized operations to round up civilians who were later executed, attacked with machetes, or raped. On several occasions rebels gave advance warning that atrocities were to be committed later. Witnesses describe the existence of distinct units for committing particular crimes like the Burn House Unit, Cut Hands Commando, and Blood Shed Squad. Some of the squads had a trademark way of killing, such as Kill Man No Blood

> Unit, whose method was to beat people to death without shedding blood, or the Born Naked Squad, who stripped their victims before killing them.[7]

All of this violence and the entrance into Freetown were broadcast globally when a journalist in the city managed to film the rebels and then the peacekeepers in action. He filmed the rebels burning a family to death in their house, having refused to become human shields, but he then also filmed paranoid Nigerian peacekeepers beating a mentally disturbed child they had mistaken for a sniper. All of this is in the seminal film *Cry Freetown*.

Following all these high-profile events, particularly the brutality of the violence visited on the civilian population, the international community was eventually spurred into action. This included the UK government: Prime Minister Tony Blair knew Sierra Leone because his father had been a school teacher there. A central group of senior UK politicians effectively decided that they could not allow the country to fall apart completely, and the UK eventually intervened militarily in 2000 when the UN peacekeepers were threatened and the UN commander in the field, General Jetley, openly accused the Nigerian troops within the previous ECOMOG (ECOWAS Monitoring Group) command of colluding with the RUF to profit from illicit diamond mining. The arrival of British troops galvanised the United Nations and secured parts of Freetown and the immediate area. It also gave confidence to the people, who promptly began demonstrating outside RUF leader Foday Sankoh's house in Freetown. Nigerian peacekeepers opened fire on the crowd, causing a surge on the house such that Sankoh's bodyguards also opened fire, Sankoh himself fleeing out of the back. The later capture of Sankoh and his incarceration by the British broke the remains of the RUF, and by July 2001 the British Expeditionary Force and the reinforced UNAMSIL (UN Mission in Sierra Leone) contingent took the offensive and gradually pacified the country.

This, then, was the overall context in which the UK intervention took place. Following the peace agreement in 2002, the UK assumed leadership of the reform process and again took up several of the threads that had been started during the war. In particular, the rebuilding of the police and military so the Sierra Leone could have some security capability became a priority. By the end of the war the UNAMSIL peacekeeping force was the biggest UN force in the field and one of the biggest ever deployed. Clearly Sierra Leone needed to develop its own capability to take over from this force. In addition there was a need for basic intelligence, since one of the key failures of the security services was that they simply had no intelligence on the RUF as it pushed towards Freetown. The new security services could not be allowed to become blind in the future.

Politics and Conflict in Sierra Leone

Since independence from Britain in 1961, the main feature of Sierra Leone's political system has been increasing centralisation of power and resources in Freetown, coupled with a deep dualism between Freetown and the rest of the country. After the rule of the Margai family ended in elections in 1967, the then mayor of Freetown, Siaka Stevens, became prime minister. Following a series of military interventions, in 1968 Stevens assumed full presidential powers and effectively held sway until his appointed successor, Major General Joseph Momoh, took over after a one-party referendum in 1985. The key feature of this period was a gradual drift towards a one-party state, increased centralisation of resources and power in Freetown and a growing alienation in the countryside and among youth in particular.

In the face of increasing political pressure, Momoh eventually established a constitutional review commission, which recommended the re-establishment of a multi-party democracy. This was approved by Parliament in July 1991. However, 1991 also saw the formation of the RUF by Foday Sankoh and increased violence along the Liberian border. The stated aim of the RUF was an end to the corrupt government of Momoh, but in reality this was quickly overtaken by a logic encompassing control of natural resources.

In Freetown, meanwhile, in 1992 another military coup brought a group of young officers headed by Valentine Strasser to power. As the leader of the National Provisional Ruling Council (NPRC), Strasser and his successors were largely ineffective, leading to an increase in the RUF's power until the involvement of the South African mercenary firm Executive Outcomes in 1995. Eventually, increasing demand in Freetown for an election, coupled with international pressure, persuaded the NPRC to hand over power to a civilian government. Following two conferences in the Bintumani Hotel in Freetown, with wide participation from civil society, elections were held in 1996; Ahmed Tejan Kabbah of the Sierra Leone People's Party (SLPP) was elected president.

Two months later, discussions between the SLPP and RUF eventually led to the Abijan Peace Accords of November 1996. The unwillingness of either party to agree to disarmament or to the international monitoring arrangements led to a breakdown of peace by early 1997. In addition, in Freetown another military coup was staged by the Armed Forces

Revolutionary Council (AFRC), and the democratically elected SLPP government was subsequent exiled to Conakry, Guinea. This, in turn, led to the next cycle of violence that culminated in the return of the SLPP government to Freetown, support from UN peacekeepers as well as UK special forces and official peace in 2002.

SSR in Sierra Leone

Since the late 1990s the post-civil war experience of Sierra Leone has become synonymous with a cluster of policies known in the international community as security sector reform. Indeed, Sierra Leone is frequently seen as *the* example of SSR, as it provides many examples of SSR best practices. It is a truism in the small world of SSR to say that there are as many different ways of undertaking it as there are contexts for doing so. Clearly any account of SSR in Sierra Leone is going to be very heavily contextualised by the situation at that time and the effects of the war. In Sierra Leone's case it also relies on a context whereby the former colonial power, the UK, intervened and was able to provide significant leadership over a long period of time. In many ways this makes Sierra Leone an exception rather than a rule, and yet this case remains important for a number of reasons, not least because if SSR fails in a state like Sierra Leone then it rather begs the question of where this particular bundle of policies might actually succeed.

The nature of this book means it is almost entirely subjective in its approach – it aims to provide a picture of what individuals were thinking about the process of SSR, not an objective analysis of data available after the event. As such it provides valuable insight into the different views and relationships that may develop during similar processes. Partly because of this, but also partly for other contextual reasons, any recommendations drawn from the experience of Sierra Leone need to viewed with caution when applied to other contexts.

There is a certain amount of contention about the labelling of SSR, and there are numerous alternatives available. While the term 'reform' remains the most common usage, we have adopted 'transformation' as a more accurate description of what actually happened in Sierra Leone. We take the view that what happened was a transformation from a non-existent security system to a functioning system, rather than a reform of an existing system. Comprehensive reform of security structures in Sierra Leone since the end of the war has spread across a wide breadth of institutions and goes to the heart of the internal and security apparatus within the country, as well as reaching out and incorporating sections of the population that had previously been subject to violence on the part of their own security services.

The Phases of Reforms in Sierra Leone

The period 1997–2007, which forms the core focus of this book, can be roughly divided into a series of distinct phases, each with its own changing set of policies and responses to a changing context.[8] This does not imply that there was no continuity between these phases, but rather that each phase tended to be set in a changing contextual situation governing the activities within that phase.

Events in the first period, 1997–2002, were determined by the overriding context of open conflict. The state of emergency in Sierra Leone at the time left no space for sitting back and developing a strategy. The country was in urgent need of support and decisions needed to be taken quickly. Programmes started in collaboration between the UK and the government of Sierra Leone were shaped as responses to consecutive crises until 2002, when the war and accompanying disarmament and demobilisation were declared over. During this period, the lack of any capacity to oversee the armed forces (which had staged two coups since 1992) and the inability to coordinate responses to security threats properly and collect intelligence were addressed by the establishment of the Sierra Leone Security Sector Reform Programme (SILSEP). Given that police primacy in addressing internal security threats had been the priority of President Kabbah since 1996, the Sierra Leone Police (SLP) were given a new ethos of local needs policing, gender-based violence was addressed through family support units, and vehicles, communication equipment and uniforms were provided. Finally, the judiciary was supported through the Law Development Programme.

At the time, as a result of the context in which operations began and because of the personalities involved, there was almost no integration of these programmes. There was no coherent concept of the security sector, and thus no organised sense of which institutions needed to be reformed. However, a general sense of direction emerged that began to take on a life of its own in subsequent phases. The initial phase until 2002 was therefore dominated by attempts to begin a security reform process in the context of fighting a war and enforcing a stuttering peace punctuated by repeated cease-fires and resumptions of conflict.

Even when the war ended officially in January 2002, there were significant areas of the countryside where conflict continued and certainly many areas that were not under the direct control of the government. The first post-war presidential and parliamentary elections were held that year, made possible by deployment of what was the biggest UN peacekeeping mission (17,000 foreign troops) to date and assisted by the SLP. The election results were a triumph for President Kabbah, who by then had come to be seen as the man who brought peace to Sierra Leone after a decade of war.

These elections marked the beginning of the second phase of Sierra Leone's security transformation process. In 2002 the nascent agencies and programmes that had helped win the war were faced with a set of challenges very different from the emergency operational planning they had conducted until then. Emerging issues included substantial rivalries between security agencies and ministries, and the thorny issue of whether the UK should continue to perform direct military operational command duties or adopt an advisory role. The government of Sierra Leone also had to deal with large numbers of armed former combatants without a functioning military and only a partly developed SLP.

An additional key development in this phase centred on producing (and linking) security strategy and development objectives for Sierra Leone. In practical terms, this was reflected in the completion of the partly interrelated poverty reduction strategy paper (PRSP) and SSR processes, where the latter was reflected in the former's Pillar One, which promotes good governance, peace and security, thus integrating security into mainstream development policy within the country.

The importance of the security sector review carried out during this period cannot be overestimated in terms of setting future policy direction. First, it gave much-needed conceptual clarity to the institutions involved in or contributing to the security sector, institutions that had a stake in defining what security meant for Sierra Leone. Second, the Office of National Security (ONS), established in 1999 as a mechanism for coordinating input from the security sector, matured during this phase and became one of the most capable and trusted security institutions in the country. Third, the fact that the security sector review was integrated into the PRSP aligned security and development to a degree that had not been done before in Sierra Leone or elsewhere.

The final period of this study, 2005–2007, was a consolidation and development phase culminating in the successful general elections of 2007. In 2005, the UK moved its Department for International Development (DFID) Sierra Leone offices from London to Freetown. One of the most important innovations of UK support for security system transformation at the time was the broadening of this support to the justice sector as a whole, rather than to the police more narrowly. Prior to the Justice Sector Development Programme (JSDP), little assistance had been given to the Ministry of Internal Affairs and prison services, in particular.

Questions regarding the future direction of security sector transformation in Sierra Leone also arose during this period. The sustainability of some of the measures deemed necessary during a war was questioned more strongly. One of the core issues was the affordability, future size and shape of the Republic of Sierra Leone Armed Forces (RSLAF). Whether the country needed a military capability at all had been questioned for many years; indeed, the security sector review produced between 2003 and 2005 identified the main threats to the country as being generated internally. Issues raised in this review continue to be of relevance.

The Structure of This Book

This volume represents one part of a broader study. The original idea for this project was to bring a set of voices into the research from those people who had been closely involved in SSR within Sierra Leone. While there may be a lot written about SSR and about Sierra Leone, as researchers we felt that there had been little attention paid to those people who had actually done it on the ground. One result of this is that the chapters are all written in very different styles. This is deliberate. The authors were tasked with the project of laying down their views of the SSR process within Sierra Leone and reflecting on the SSR process from a variety of different viewpoints.

Another element that needs clarification is that these chapters represent slightly different perspectives at differing times in the process. Although the authors have all given overviews of their own areas, the phase of the reform process they were involved with has clearly coloured their experience. This work is no less valuable for that, but these documents do represent primary evidence from on the ground and need to be viewed and judged in that light.

Part II comprises five chapters from UK government personnel and consultants who were engaged in the process at particular times. Robert Ashington-Pickett was involved at the very early stages of intelligence reform in Sierra Leone, and his chapter is critical in setting the scene for those who were given instructions in Whitehall and then had to adapt to local needs and the local context on the ground. It also emphasises the central role of intelligence reform and the ONS in the entire SSR process.

Barry Le Grys's chapter outlines the UK approach to military involvement, particularly through the International Military Advisory Training Team (IMATT), and the continuing issues surrounding relationships between UK forces and the RSLAF. He brings an invaluable insight culled from a long-term interest in the country, serving under UN command during 2001 and then as military adviser to the government of Sierra Leone and IMATT commander in 2006. Another side of this military involvement is reviewed by Aldo Gaeta, who was posted inside the MoD and was engaged in developing civil-military relations and civil service systems of oversight, budgeting and planning. In particular, he draws on his experiences of providing logistical support and barracks to the military within the country and gives an insight into the difficulties of establishing a working system when trust between civil and military authorities had broken down.

Mark White was a DFID adviser in Sierra Leone, and his chapter concentrates on the interconnections and disjuncture between security and development within the SSR process. While is has become a cliché to talk about 'no development without security and no security without development', this gets to the core of the relationship between the two, outlining the problematic relationship and showing that while significant progress has been made since 1999 in ensuring that security and development are interrelated, there is still some way to go before they are fully integrated into either policy or programmatic practice. Clearly this chapter is of significant interest not only to those analysing the experience of Sierra Leone but also for those engaged in such linked development and security programmes in countries as diverse as Iraq and Afghanistan.

Finally from the UK side, there is a comprehensive chapter from Anthony Howlett-Bolton looking at the development of justice interventions and the relationships. This chapter aims to develop discussion surrounding the need to ensure holistic development approaches for both justice and security sectors whilst also documenting justice and security sector progress in Sierra Leone from 1999 to 2007. Given the dominant influence of the security sector, which appears sometimes to attempt to subsume the justice sector, or at least portray it as a junior partner, this chapter reflects the general approach of the Sierra Leone Justice Sector Development Programme (JSDP) by raising the profile of justice sector development whilst concentrating on those elements specifically allied to security.

Part III of the book comprises six chapters from Sierra Leoneans who have been involved in the process of security reconstruction for some time. It is one of the key characteristics of the reform process during this ten-year period that the Sierra Leonean team remained stable relative to the UK protagonists, who mainly (but not exclusively) operated on shorter-term contracts and frequently changed.

This section starts with the critical issue of governance and governance reform. Emmanuel Osho Coker's chapter outlines the critical context of governance reforms within a post-conflict environment, and further identifies key issues and challenges involved with rebuilding a government effectively from scratch. One notable aspect is the discussion about the relationship between those public servants within the MoD and the military and those excluded from the SSR process. The government clearly had to maintain a balance between getting good people into post while at the same time maintaining a degree of equity across the civil service system, and the chapter illustrates some of the issues involved in achieving this.

The following two chapters document the development of the military in the country and its institutional and legal context. Nelson-Williams outlines the nature of the changes and discussions surrounding the military and the role of IMATT within the RSALF. Kondeh moves this discussion on to cover some of the legal and policy aspects of restructuring militaries, including the development of a white paper and a working MoD. These reforms within the military are complemented by Kadi Fakondo's chapter on the reform and reconstruction of the Sierra Leonean Police and the rather different strategy adopted by UK advisers within the SLP.

Conteh's chapter looks at the development of the ONS as an overarching security institution and a key vehicle for developing a strategic overview of the actual security situation and the main issues concerning the population in general. Within this, the development of a decentralised system of provincial and district security committees allowed the construction of a meaningful security sector review. At the same time, the development of civil society and the role played by civil society groups in the articulation of some of these policies was central to the success of part of the reform. Hanson-Alp's chapter documents the difficulties, challenges and successes of this process, and many of the elements discussed here will be familiar to readers. In particular, the role played by civil society in the oversight of security forces is put at the heart of this discussion, which raises several challenging points.

The book finishes with an overview chapter that attempts to provide a clear framework and analysis of all of the reforms in a holistic way. In particular, the chapter tries to assess whether or not the reform process itself was a success, and if so, how much of a success. It also outlines the remaining key issues and what still needs to be done, concluding that while there have been successes, the experience of Sierra Leone remains very much an exception rather than a rule: some of the things that Sierra Leone experienced – a long-term memorandum of understanding, clear lead donor – do not exist in many other countries. Most importantly of all, the chapter concludes that despite all the investment and effort over such a long time, the process remains unfinished. While there are functioning security services, the more difficult elements of political and civil control and oversight remain relatively undeveloped, leading to a situation where a withdrawal by the UK government could be a considerable political risk. Finally the chapter outlines some of the potential ways forward, concluding that Sierra Leone has had significant success, but work remains.

Notes

1 Available at http://hdrestats.undp.org/en/countries/country_fact_sheets/cty_fs_SLE.html (accessed 29 January 2010).

2 Kaplan, Robert (1994) 'The coming anarchy: How scarcity, crime, overpopulation and disease are rapidly destroying the social fabric of our planet', *Atlantic Monthly*, 273(2): 44–76.

3 Ibid.: 45.

4 See for example Richards, Paul (1998) *Fighting for the Rain Forest, Youth and Resources in Sierra Leone*, Oxford: James Currey; Gberie, Lans (2005) *A Dirty War in West Africa: The RUF and the Destruction of Sierra Leone*, Bloomington, IN: Indiana University Press; Keen, David (2005) *Conflict and Collusion in Sierra Leone,* Oxford: James Currey.

5 Richards, ibid.; Keen, ibid.

6 It is no accident that Foday Sankoh became minister for mineral resources in Sierra Leone towards the end of the conflict.

7 Human Rights Watch (1999) *Getting Away With Murder, Mutilation and Rape*, New York: HRW.

8 We have documented these phases in some detail in Jackson, P. and Albrecht, P. (2009) *Security Sector Transformation in Sierra Leone 1997–2007*, Birmingham: DFID/GFN-SSR.

Part II

UK Perspectives

Chapter 2

Intelligence and Security Service Reconstruction

Robert Ashington-Pickett

Introduction

This chapter outlines a number of the key aspects of building an intelligence and security service (ISS) as part of the Sierra Leone Security Sector Programme (SILSEP) from 2000 to 2003. The ISS reform experience in Sierra Leone was unique for various reasons. First, these reforms were essentially initiated during a time of war; thus capacity-building processes and delivery of intelligence products were carried out simultaneously. Second, the ISS reform programme had an unusual funding structure. Thirdly, there were in general great sensitivities regarding capacity-building of intelligence services, particularly since the country was just emerging from conflict.

The chapter will discuss these and other issues, and suggest key lessons learned that may benefit similar processes in other post-conflict contexts. It will also demonstrate, based on the author's practical experience, that security sector reform (SSR) in general, and ISS in particular, are inherently political and specific to context.

Background

The ISS element of SSR in Sierra Leone emerged out of the military SILSEP project. SILSEP focused on restructuring the Sierra Ministry of Defence (MoD), and was conceived as a complement to military reforms led by the UK International Military Assistance Training Team (IMATT). At the same time, the Lomé Peace Agreement made provision for the post-war restructuring of the RSLAF, providing an international legal framework for the interventions by the UK. As part of this effort, it was agreed that SILSEP would also need to work within State House, the building of the executive, to ensure that parallel reforms would take place at the senior government, service and ministry levels. In 1999 the head of the SILSEP team was tasked to concentrate on developing and supporting the function of the Sierra Leone national security adviser.

Despite difficult circumstances, progress was made during 1999–2000 in establishing a number of key platforms on which later success was built. With additional support and direction from a visiting UK intelligence adviser, SILSEP began to contribute towards a functioning National Security Council (NSC), the outline of a National Security Act and the drafting of a national security policy.

However, it also became clear during this period that SSR within the national security and intelligence sphere needed to be considered as a separate activity and not just an adjunct to the development project in the MoD. In 2000 the UK Department for International Development (DFID) established a separate ISS programme to balance the programmes in the MoD, armed forces and police. It concluded that this ISS programme would require a full-time adviser with both a government intelligence background and an understanding of capacity-building, development and other related issues. To this end, the former UK army officer who had been covering the embryonic ISS was replaced by a professional intelligence officer with experience in organisational development.

With the latter's arrival in January 2001, the ISS element of SILSEP acquired an identity separate from the MoD programme (by that time known as MODAT, the Ministry of Defence Assistance Team) and a distinct ISS strategy emerged.

At the same time, a concept of ISS reform was taking shape in DFID in London around the core functions of 'all-source intelligence assessment' and security coordination. Guided by advisers from the UK intelligence establishment, DFID was on a steep learning curve. It had begun to recognise that certain national security functions are critical to central government; in particular, they are important ingredients in the constitution of an effective NSC. At this stage, however, the question of improving the efficiency and effectiveness of collecting agencies was still not addressed; neither were other ISS issues, such as the policy advice function, national crisis management and a number of other functions which were later to become SILSEP issues. As a result, the scope of the ISS element was underestimated and initial resources allocated to the new intelligence and security adviser (ISA) were soon to prove insufficient for the task ahead. The objectives assigned to the ISA were:

- Create an all-source intelligence assessment capability
- Shepherd the passing of the National Security and Central Intelligence Act
- Develop secretariat support for the National Security Council
- Support the development of the role of national security adviser
- Make the collecting agencies more accountable and transparent
- Establish a central, provincial and district security coordination capacity

This, therefore, was the skeleton of an ISS SSR strategy, although it lacked many connecting rods, and above all lacked an understanding of the key task of creating a fully functioning intelligence-collection capacity on which all else would be based.

Fortunately, as the greater remit of the programme became clearer, funding became available from the Africa Conflict Prevention Pool, while DFID provided two more advisers to support the ISA in late 2002. These advisers worked on a part-time basis and concentrated on particularly resource-intensive areas such as intelligence assessment processes and development of detailed standard operating procedures.

Nurturing National Leadership for SSR Actions

Good process, technology, and funding cannot compensate for fundamental failings in human capacity. In taking forward an ISS SSR programme, the human dimension is particularly important, whether it concerns the expertise and behaviour of the SSR programme manager/advisers or the individuals who are to staff the reformed security institutions. This aspect is, however, easily overlooked, and there is often pressure to implement SSR programmes without making sufficient effort to identify individuals and match them with the tasks at hand.

Clearly there was an issue with leadership across a number of security institutions. Brigadier General Maxwell Kbobe (Nigerian) was installed as the chief of defence staff and Commander Keith Biddle, a British police officer, became a senior figure within the Sierra Leone Police (SLP). There was a lack of experience among senior Sierra Leonean officers in running and coordinating security and intelligence organisations.

Considerable effort was made early on to replace unsuitable individuals, which diverted time and energy that could have been better spent in other pursuits. However, this effort later produced benefits, especially when compared with other government departments which had not taken, or were prevented from taking, steps to assure appropriate staffing. This was also an early indicator that the SSR programme existed in an intensely political environment, and that management of the political dimension would be critical to the programme's success.

In particular, the appointment of the national security coordinator and the head of the Central Intelligence and Security Unit (CISU) proved to be extremely beneficial in providing longer-term leadership for their respective organisations.

Institutional Reforms

CISU and collecting agencies

At the restart of SILSEP in early 2000, there were apparently three intelligence-collecting agencies: the SLP Special Branch (SB), the Military Intelligence Branch (MIB) and CISU, formerly existing under the name of the National Intelligence Unit. Of these, only CISU was new; while it had been established in the pre-2000 phase of SILSEP, it had existed largely on paper and only its director was capable of operational activity.

The first meeting of the Joint Intelligence Committee (JIC) in 2000 concluded that radical restructuring of all three collecting agencies was necessary in order to achieve a workable level of intelligence production and, in turn, provide the JIC with reliable and actionable intelligence. This meant that a new and substantial task had already emerged, but it was equally clear that there was no point in building capacity in the JIC and creating a joint assessment centre if there was no usable intelligence for them to assess and action.

This call for improved intelligence gathering immediately caused problems for programme management, since the original timetable and resource allocation had not foreseen the need to develop intelligence-collection capacity. Furthermore, this created institutional problems for DFID, since it did not believe that developing such operational capacity was part of its charter.

In the event, it was agreed that the UK intelligence community would support development of operational capability in parallel with SILSEP development of analytical and other downstream 'non-operational' capacities. This operational capacity-building was aimed primarily at CISU, although the SLP-SB and MIB were also beneficiaries, largely by participating in various training programmes. This development activity was funded separately out of the Africa Conflict Prevention Pool.

This was no small matter. This response to identification of an additional development task demonstrated how progress could be made by applying flexible and creative thinking and adopting a collaborative approach. It was achieved, in part, by the fortunate ability of key UK players, the SLP-SB and MIB advisers and the ISA, all of whom had considerable inter-agency experience in their former government positions, to work together and agree on a set of common objectives.

In fact, early in the ISS process the ISA and UK advisers to the SLP-SB and MIB made an informal agreement to seek every opportunity to collaborate and share resources. This, in turn, led to Sierra Leonean members of the three collecting agencies gradually overcoming traditional and deep-rooted suspicions, learning to collaborate with their colleagues and thus creating a sense of a Sierra Leonean intelligence community. It is important to note that where shared experience of inter-agency cooperation did not exist, coordination and agreement between wider SSR strands appeared to be weaker.

Office of National Security and the national security coordinator

The coming together of the new national security adviser and the UK's ISA in early 2000 provided an opportunity to rethink the national security architecture and early assumptions. This had several major outcomes.

- Depersonalisation: the new national security adviser (formally personal adviser to the president and supported by his secretariat) became the national security coordinator and head of the new Office of National Security (ONS).
- Depoliticisation: systematic removal of party politics (and politicians) from the ONS and CISU was an obvious necessity. These organisations would primarily support the rule of law and protect the constitution, not individuals, parties or tribal groupings.
- Separation of clandestine intelligence operations (CISU) from intelligence assessment and security policy advice (ONS).
- UK advisers would not function independently of their Sierra Leonean counterparts, but in support of them. Therefore, the ISA would only meet with the president in the company (and with the support) of the national security coordinator and director general of CISU.

- Quality over quantity: organisations would grow in line with their ability to absorb growth and internalise guiding SSR principles. It was agreed that a small number of carefully selected and trained individuals would be better than a large number of unsuited and insufficiently trained individuals.
- Involvement of civil society and provincial authorities: the ONS would be the interface between the security apparatus and general society and would extend this role to the provincial and district levels.
- Government agency (as opposed to department) status for both ONS and CISU: the more flexible agency status allowed for necessary increased levels of protective and information security as compared to the rest of the civil service, and more suitable terms and conditions of employment.
- Conduct of needed security and intelligence activity without waiting for the rest of the civil service to catch up with its own reforms.
- Continued linkage of the ONS and CISU to wider governance reforms while they remained integral and accountable branches of government service.

While these points may seem self-evident and unremarkable in retrospect, it is worth remembering that at the time each point was innovative and critical to future success and sustainability of the programme.

Other government departments

It was accepted early on that national security should be viewed 'holistically'. This approach was included in the first draft of the national security policy and signified that national security was part of and not separate from wider aspects of government activity, economics and civil society. This philosophical position had many implications, not least of which was the inclusion of other government departments (OGDs) in various aspects of security strategy and policy advice and formulation. Unfortunately, the uneven pace of reform elsewhere in the Sierra Leone government did not allow integration of government activity to occur seamlessly. For example, at first the JIC did not permanently include officials from, say, the Ministry of Foreign Affairs, nor did it allow for attachments from OGDs to the ONS.

There were, however, some welcome and early exceptions to this. In late 2001, for example, the Anti-corruption Commission sent an observer to the JIC, a move which enabled the commission to inform SSR of wider corruption developments as well as to receive practical support from the Sierra Leone security sector. Furthermore, by late 2002 it was increasingly possible and productive to invite members of OGDs to take part in JIC meetings discussing issues of interest to that department and for ONS analysts to visit OGDs for research purposes.

Capacity-Building and the Three Variables

According to one widely accepted theory of organisational development, there are three variables present in developing capacity in an organisation; success depends on balancing and integrating the three.

People

As mentioned above, it was agreed within the ISS part of SILSEP that resolving the human aspects of the programme satisfactorily constituted a *sine qua non*. While considerable political effort was expended ensuring that only suitable individuals were to staff the executive levels of CISU and ONS, similar efforts were made to recruit suitable new entrants to staff the organisations from the bottom up. This meant avoiding the trap of importing new entrants wholesale from, say, the armed services, police or the *ad hoc* organisation that formed the Sierra Leone government in Conakry.[1] It also meant avoiding pressure from inside and outside Sierra Leone to create a fully staffed (but dysfunctional) organisation as quickly as possible.

Despite initial scepticism, events were to demonstrate that a small number of carefully selected, well-suited and well-trained officers were far more effective than a large number of unsuitable and unqualified staff members. Such appointments also facilitated genuine attainment of many core SSR principles more easily than otherwise might have been the case.

It was therefore agreed to take time to create a talent-spotting, screening and recruitment mechanism in keeping with the ethical, intellectual and physical demands of the new organisations. To achieve this, the principles behind recruitment methods for UK intelligence agencies were adapted to suit Sierra Leone conditions and the process was submitted to the Sierra Leone Establishment secretary and the Civil Service Commission for approval (i.e. there was no circumventing of Sierra Leone government procedures). Following the recruitment process, all staff members were given formal training by UK intelligence officers in the basic principles of intelligence direction, collection and analysis. This included members of the ONS, on the basis that a good understanding of this function was important to their subsequent roles in all-source assessment and security coordination. CISU officers were then provided with more advanced training in their chosen areas of expertise, while ONS officers received separate coaching in their subject areas. This training was probably less satisfactory concerning intelligence assessment, largely because of a lack of suitable courses and trainers in this specialised area.

In keeping with the guiding principle of inter-agency cooperation, Sierra Leone nationals from the SLP-SB, MIB and, later, the Anti-corruption Commission were invited to take part in the courses. This broader training proved to be effective, as it broke down barriers to effective collaboration and gained more training 'bangs for bucks'. In those areas where there was a clear operational aspect to the training, funding was provided by the Africa Conflict Prevention Pool rather than by DFID development funds.

Technology (buildings and equipment)

In Sierra Leone in 2000, when war effectively remained a reality, suitable office buildings were in short supply. Nevertheless, the ONS and CISU were allocated a wing on the State House site, which conveyed certain advantages (including proximity to the new MoD across the street). However, the location was not well suited to the needs of restrictive security, and caused initial confusion within CISU and ONS over their separate identities.

With considerable assistance from SILSEP funds, it was possible to make the offices serviceable and relatively secure. Emphasis was placed on ease of maintenance, physical security and functionality. This meant that a relatively low-tech IT approach was adopted. This allowed for ease of maintenance and information assurance, which would not have been the case with the more costly option of local area network (LAN) and wide area network (WAN) systems. LAN/WAN could not be easily supported within Sierra Leone at that time, and would have been vulnerable to hostile penetration.

Limited funding for vehicles, combined with the needs of protective security, led to the decision to purchase an assortment of low-profile used vehicles rather than an even smaller number of high-profile new vehicles.

In CISU, meanwhile, the difficulties of DFID in funding operational requirements were overcome by separate access to funding from the Africa Conflict Prevention Pool. This allowed for a minimum level of equipment purchases, including photographic and vision-enhancement tools, intelligence analysis software and training.

Policy and procedures

The next critical step in capacity-building is the development of a structure of policy and procedures, which constitutes the framework within which the organisation operates. This includes standard operating procedures, which provide guidance for safe and secure daily operations of the organisation and the rules by which it functions. Done properly, development of policy and procedures will promote more effective service delivery, help safeguard key SSR principles, give direction to the staff members and improve operational safety and security. It was important to SILSEP that these policies and procedures be developed in parallel with other capacity-building areas and that they be locally owned and not simply 'cut and paste' from some other part of the world. Again, this implies more effort and time, but the benefits are many, including greater sustainability and compliance.

In general, institutional policies and procedures begin with national legislation to establish legal parameters. When the 2002 Sierra Leone National Security and Central Intelligence Act was passed, it established ISS legal parameters, including the organisations' responsibilities, authority, resources and limits. These legislative boundaries were then translated into standard operating procedures and CISU and ONS staff regulations.

The ISS approach was to develop and draft policies and procedures in response to events and capacity-building efforts, and involve Sierra Leone partners in the process. This led to the gradual evolution of local, rather than external, standard operating policies and procedures. In retrospect, this activity initially lagged behind others, largely because of the size of the task. The project did not begin to make good this shortfall until the arrival of one of the additional part-time ISA advisers in the second half of 2002.

SSR Context

Many of the environmental factors affecting SSR programmes in other states were present in Sierra Leone. Because these factors represent additional complexity and ambiguity, there is, perhaps, a desire to ignore them or reduce their significance.

Vested interests

In Sierra Leone, because of perceived threats to vested interests, there was considerable opposition to many aspects of SSR, including national security legislation. As often happens, many stakeholders were supportive of SSR in principle, but opposed many of its details.

Similarly, a perception trap can operate whereby principal stakeholders agree to SSR but frequently have a different idea of what it means. These different perceptions can lead to the expectation that SSR will make security agencies:

- More effective at doing what they are already doing
- Able to do things that they currently cannot (but which might be wrong)
- Cost less
- Or any combination of the above, while key SSR principles are overlooked or ignored

This was the case with SILSEP. At a general level, vested interests are threatened by ISS SSR in the following situations.

1. A group or individual wishes to retain control over part or all of the security apparatus as a means to extend its/their power.
2. A reformed and independent security apparatus threatens to reveal and oppose a group or individual's illegitimate activities (especially corruption).
3. A more effective security apparatus threatens to identify the shortcomings of another organisation or individual.
4. A more effective intelligence machinery demands better policy-making and highlights inadequacies.

This list is not exhaustive, but it indicates that in the course of an SSR programme there can be many who would wish to obstruct progress for reasons which are not immediately obvious. Many of the individuals threatened may be those who populate the local political landscape and who fear that reformed security agencies will no longer be available to serve their personal and/or political purposes. The list of opponents may also include external actors, such as donor project managers, who identify too narrowly with the organisation they are advising and view other SSR programmes as competitors for donor resources or internal political influence. This was a feature of SSR that was not at all well understood at the outset of the programme, and only imperfectly understood at the end of the period in question here.

Legislation

The question of national security legislation, including its conception, drafting, the consultation process and its parliamentary passage, is worth separate and detailed consideration. It is sufficient to note here that the legislative model used in Sierra Leone was not taken from the UK, but from a number of other African countries and heavily adapted for Sierra Leone with a number of innovative features. The entire legislative project was expertly supported by the Sierra Leone legal draftsman.

The legislation's slow passage through government was unexpectedly instructive, as it exposed some of the vested interests discussed above. This slow passage may also have reflected discomfort within the establishment regarding defining the roles and limitations of ISS organisations while also establishing their political independence. As a result, the National Security and Central Intelligence Act experienced delays ranging from the sophisticated to the banal. These included repeated delays in both finding space on the parliamentary agenda and obtaining executive sign-off. One of the final obstacles was the apparent lack of the right sort of paper on which to print it. Despite all this, it did finally become an exemplary piece of primary security sector legislation, embodying principles of transparency, democratic oversight, accountability and separation of powers in a manageable and readable form that was accessible and comprehensible to the people.

Collapse/absence of public administration

A common challenge facing SSR and governance programmes in post-conflict societies is the lack of administrative foundation. SSR programme design in Sierra Leone had made certain reasonable assumptions about other elements of public administration being in place. However, while these administrative elements may appear on paper, they often have little substance. SSR advisers often have to track well beyond their project to find firm administrative foundations upon which to build.

For example, the ISS found that administrative mechanisms for civil service screening and recruitment were inadequate; the task of creating such mechanisms to organise staffing of the ONS and CISU fell to the programme

among SSR advisers and overprotectiveness of one's agency or department. At times, this behaviour is imported into post-conflict arenas where it creates a new arena for rivalries to be played out, thus undermining key SSR principles and setting a bad example. While SSR programmes in Sierra Leone benefited from the aforementioned professional behaviour, they still suffered from inter-agency rivalries and turf battles.

This situation is not, however, inevitable. The risks associated with 'silo thinking' can be substantially mitigated by:

- Careful selection of SSR advisers to screen out those with prejudices against inter-department cooperation and seek those with a positive track record of working in multi-agency and multinational environments
- Integrated local and UK command, control, communication and intelligence structures to manage and coordinate the range of SSR projects (replacing stovepipe reporting lines back to the UK)
- Creation of SSR team spirit before deployment
- Formal, inter-programme objectives (e.g. concerning corruption and governance)

Making it Work

SSR in conflict

A key feature of Sierra Leone's SSR process was that it evolved during a conflict. This meant that the requirement for products from the central national security coordination function (ONS) and the intelligence service (CISU) predated the existence of these organisations. This created a situation in which senior political figures and organisations, not least the embryonic National Security Council, expected that intelligence would be available, assessments made, policy advice submitted and strategy drafted from the moment the first makeshift office signs were hung on the State House doors. This placed a heavy burden on those who staffed those offices: they had to create organisations and deliver products simultaneously. Clearly, this was an unrealistic expectation that would not occur in analogous organisations in donor countries, but this circle needed to be squared, somehow, in Sierra Leone.

It is important to point out here the difference between this 'create and produce' environment and circumstances surrounding other organisations undergoing fundamental changes.

- Reforming a dysfunctional but existing organisation: for example, the Sierra Leone Police. In this case the reforming organisation was required to improve on an already existing capability (however limited and flawed that capacity might have been).
- Forming a new organisation from existing functional organisations: for example, the Serious Organised Crime Agency in the UK. In this case the new organisation could draw on experienced and qualified individuals who had functioned in similar roles before.

This is not to say that these tasks are any easier; but they are different and require different approaches. In the first case, building capacity in a dysfunctional but existing organisation may concentrate more on retraining existing human capacity and steadily improving service delivery from a low but acceptable starting point. In the second case, forming a new organisation from existing functional organisations might focus more on breaking down former inter-agency rivalries, creating a new corporate identity and refining organisational structures.

In the case of the ONS and CISU, there was neither a pre-existing organisational capacity on which to build nor a body of trained and experienced individuals to draw upon and merge. To deliver against the expectations outlined above, the ONS and CISU needed to establish an interim capability to service the immediate needs of both the government and its international partners. This was crucial, but did take time away from basic capacity-building.

The pressure of these expectations placed senior ONS and CISU officials in something of a 'lose/lose' situation. The development lobby accused them of not prioritising capacity-building and reform. The government and the war-fighting lobby accused them of not prioritising delivery of intelligence material/operations and national security advice.

These challenges were not well understood at the time and could have led to failure. However, both ONS and CISU officials managed to perform a difficult balancing act: both service delivery and reform agendas were able to move forward, although not without disappointing different lobbies at various times.

Building capacity and relevance: SSR and war-fighting

When discussing the more arcane and academic aspects of SSR, it is perhaps easy to lose sight of the fact that security sector agencies are called upon to undertake work that is frequently dangerous. This is particularly so when the country is engaged in armed conflict, as was Sierra Leone for much of the period under review.

In the author's view, there is an implicit responsibility on the part of SSR projects to reduce risks to life that are inherent in the security context. This view was certainly shared by other SSR advisers in Sierra Leone during this period.

The intelligence-gathering mission of CISU, for example, required penetration of paramilitary forces known for extremely violent behaviour. Such operations are dangerous. One of the features of good management of intelligence operations is operational security, which reduces risks to an acceptable minimum. This capacity takes time and experience to build. CISU was faced with the challenge of running such operations before operational security capacity was sufficiently developed; it responded to the issue by providing UK advisers to vet and oversee such operations without becoming actively involved in the operations themselves. While this might have involved a more interventionist approach than otherwise desirable or necessary, experience suggests that it was the right and responsible approach and should be recognised as a feature of ISS SSR programmes.

This style of adviser mentoring was known in the project as the 'driving instructor' approach. It allowed a certain amount of adviser intervention to avoid a serious crash and permitted our Sierra Leonean colleagues to maintain full control of organisation and operations.

Intelligence operations

The requirements of restrictive security necessarily limit comprehensive discussion of the contribution of CISU and other intelligence agencies to the defeat of the Revolutionary United Front (RUF) and the establishment of security in post-conflict Sierra Leone. However, no mention of this would leave the question of the value of ISS SSR incomplete.

CISU, despite its small size, was able to make a substantial contribution to understanding the intentions and capacities of the RUF leadership and to have an impact on the will of that leadership to maintain armed conflict. CISU and its partners were also able to contribute to an understanding and tracking of the other hostile and destabilising forces in

Sierra Leone and neighbouring countries. This intelligence was shared with Sierra Leone's allies and was considered to be of good value.

Also of considerable value was the new ability of the reformed security sector to evaluate outside sources of information for the government, in particular for the office of the president. In many cases these outside sources were evaluated as peddling disinformation or rumour; good evaluation by CISU and others helped prevent inappropriate government actions and responses.

Security coordination and policy advice

Similarly, in its infancy the ONS needed to improve security coordination and decision-making within government and with external actors such as the UK government and the UN Mission in Sierra Leone (UNAMSIL). Moreover, it also had the considerable logistical challenge of establishing its relevance and achieving regionial security coordination through the establishment of provincial security committees (PROSECs) and district security committees (DISECs).

The establishment of PROSECs and DISECs was considered important in extending the national security coordination function beyond the central government in Freetown and involving the entire country in security governance. Broader security governance would also result in:

- Increased local government and community cooperation with the security agencies
- More efficient cooperation between the security agencies
- Improved quality of information passed on to central government

The relative delay in establishing PROSECs and DISECs was not due to underestimating their importance, but rather to the lack of central capacity to staff, fund and manage them and the need first to create a solid, central national security function to which regional bodies would report.

One notable national security innovation was the establishment of the National Security Council Coordinating Group (NSCCG), a Sierra Leone-generated solution for the challenges it faced from 2002 onwards. This mechanism could well have application in other SSR programmes. The NSCCG's aim was to establish a high-level coordinating group of the most senior security officials from the government, the UK and the UN. This enabled analysis of information from all available sources and consequent policy advice, which could then be submitted for approval within the respective organisations. In particular, this analysis would provide clear direction to the NSC and the president. The NSCCG filled the perceived gap between the political decision-makers, technical experts and operators.

Conclusion

This chapter has presented key aspects of the ISS SSR process in Sierra Leone during the period from 2000 to 2003. It has discussed some of the complications, challenges and successes that the author encountered while assisting in the establishment of the ONS and CISU. Remember that Sierra Leone was still at war as the ISS SSR process began; this meant that the functions of ONS and CISU were needed before these organisations had been fully established. It was also clear that, given its involvement in building intelligence community capacity, the UK government was charting new territory.

Upon arriving in Sierra Leone, the ISA found that he was working within the context of a number of assumptions held by many stakeholders, not least the donors. The most significant of these were as follows.

1. National security and intelligence organisations are inherently undemocratic, unaccountable and not transparent; there is therefore a conflict between increasing effectiveness and increasing accountability and transparency. It was implicitly accepted that a principal task of any ISS SSR programme was to 'rein in' such organisations. In fact, this assumption was critically flawed and created a negative starting point from which to run such a programme. Much else follows on from this assumption, so it is important to get it right.
2. ISS functions are not interdependent: for example, it is possible to build a central intelligence assessment group without building the capacity to deliver reliable intelligence to such a group.
3. Success would be achieved by creating a scaled-down replica of the UK intelligence machinery.
4. It was necessary to accept and work with all the individuals who the host nation had originally allocated to the organisations.
5. It was necessary to compromise on certain basic practices of running an effective intelligence organisation (e.g. screening and vetting processes) because local circumstances would not allow them or there was insufficient time to implement such practices.

6. The various SSR programmes did not need to be carefully coordinated.
7. SSR was a technical development activity and did not possess any substantial political dimension.
8. SSR was a development activity much like any other, and did not require any additional protective security measures for those carrying it out.

All these assumptions were later found to be flawed; but before that realisation occurred, much opportunity, energy and time were lost.

Among the many aspects of the ISS process, two are paramount and sometimes easily forgotten. One is the critical role of people and the fact that good processes, skeletal institutions, technical assistance and funding cannot compensate for fundamental failings in human capacity. The human dimension is critical, and this applies to both international advisers and local individuals who will be staffing the institution in question. Though this appears somewhat of a truism, it is often overlooked. Without the right people to sustain technical processes that are being put in place, these efforts will be in vain. The current status of the ONS and CISU as two of the most effective and accountable institutions in Sierra Leone's security sector is very much a testament to their staff.

Second, the vested interests of certain groups or individuals can amount to resistance to the SSR process as a whole. Ultimately, this speaks to the inherently political nature of SSR. Many aspects of SSR in Sierra Leone encountered considerable opposition, for instance with respect to outlining clearly the remits of the intelligence agencies in national security legislation. It is not uncommon that support is given to the principles and framework of SSR while actual implementation is opposed.

Note

1 The democratically elected Sierra Leone government, run by the Sierra Leone People's Party, was exiled to Conakry, Guinea, in 1997, when the Armed Forces Revolutionary Council (AFRC) staged a coup. The government returned to power in 1998.

Chapter 3

British Military Involvement in Sierra Leone, 2001–2006

Barry J. Le Grys

Introduction

The aim of this chapter is to examine progress in Sierra Leone between 2001 and 2006, within a regional context, as a result of UK military intervention and assistance. It focuses on what is commonly termed post-conflict reconstruction and development. In particular, it will explore the transformation of the security sector[1] and the relationship between security and development.

The chapter draws on research, but also on first-hand experience of the author, who served in Sierra Leone under UN command during 2001 and then as military adviser to the government of Sierra Leone (GoSL) and commander of the International Military Advisory Training Team (IMATT) in 2006.

Security Arrives (eventually)

Civil war broke out in Sierra Leone in 1991 when the Revolutionary United Front (RUF) entered the country from Liberia in the east. The bitter struggle continued until an apparent truce in 1999 (the Lomé Agreement). UN Security Council Resolution 1270 established the UN Mission in Sierra Leone (UNAMSIL) to oversee the agreement. The UN force was to relieve a force from the Economic Community of West African States (ECOWAS) that had been mandated by the UN in 1997 to restore Ahmad Tejan Kabbah to power (he was elected president in 1996, but removed by a coup the following year). The troubles experienced by the ECOWAS force were passed on to the UN, whose blue-helmet troops came under attack as soon as ECOWAS troops departed in April 2000. The RUF once again threatened to overrun the capital, Freetown; the UN mission was in severe jeopardy. A UK military force, originally ordered to conduct an evacuation of British nationals, intervened decisively and turned the RUF back in 2000. UN and UK forces then cooperated to establish security. While the UN focused upon peacebuilding, UK forces concentrated on rebuilding state security structures. The war was officially declared over in 2002, and Kabbah won the presidential elections in the same year.

While the RUF ceased hostilities in 2001, there were sporadic local outbreaks of violence. UNAMSIL was regaining confidence, rebalancing and building strength after earlier, almost catastrophic, setbacks. But since a great deal of the country was not under GoSL civil authority, UNAMSIL's access and freedom of movement were restricted. Makeni was largely under RUF control, Kabala was surrounded by the RUF and Koidu was in RUF hands. The UN accepted a UK offer of seven military officers to serve with the UN force headquarters in Freetown. Their primary task was to reinforce UNAMSIL's inadequate planning capability; their secondary task was to ensure that coordination with the UK joint task force was seamless. The result of this infusion was a far better collaborative effort to roll out security across the country. Ties between UNAMSIL's provision of wider area security and support, the UK-led Sierra Leone Army (SLA) and the Sierra Leone Police (SLP) were greatly strengthened.

The most significant move forward for UNAMSIL was the implementation of a plan to put a coherent, one-nation, combined-arms brigade into the east of the country, centred on Koidu. After a tremendous diplomatic effort involving Freetown, New York, Washington, London and Islamabad, Pakistan provided the required brigade. The psychological effect on the RUF of a UK-sponsored SLA advancing from the west and a robust UN brigade in the heart of its revenue source was hugely positive. Violent confrontation was no longer an option for the RUF. At this early stage of emerging stability, the concept of SLP primacy for internal security was instigated. UNAMSIL conducted joint patrols with the SLP, while the SLA was encouraged to defend the border and guard against external threats. Civil authority, at the time more a case of show rather than substance, was established as Sierra Leone's districts were disarmed. Illegal arms caches were sought out by SLP cordon and search operations, supported by SLA and UNAMSIL troops.

National Security in Sierra Leone (so far, so good)

There are signs that security sector reform (SSR) in Sierra Leone has been relatively successful. UNAMSIL, which numbered some 17,000 troops at its height, withdrew in 2005; the primary responsibility for internal security now lies with the SLP. A security sector review[2] has been undertaken and is linked to the country's 2005 poverty reduction strategy paper (PRSP). This review's recommendations are now being implemented, albeit slowly due to a severe lack of funding.

The reality and perception of security in Sierra Leone are seen as indispensable for the growth of domestic economic activity as well as for increased foreign investment. This is a key theme of Pillar One of the PRSP, which states 'good governance, consolidated peace and a strengthened security sector are key elements of the enabling environment for delivery of services for attainment of food security, creation of employment opportunities, human development and economic growth'.[3] To date, the UK has invested heavily in Pillar One, including substantial funding of the security sector. As part of the SSR process, the National Security and Central Intelligence Act was passed in 2002, leading to the establishment of the Office of National Security (ONS) and the Central Intelligence and Security Unit (CISU). The ONS, a post-conflict innovation, is responsible for ensuring joint sector-wide assessments on a regular basis and coordinating the activities of the security agencies. It serves as the secretariat to the National Security Council (NSC), which is chaired by the president.

The ONS also sponsors provincial and subordinate district security committees (PROSECs and DISECs) that allow local community involvement in threat assessment and risk management. These are formal regional forums established to bring together primary security players, local government, civil society representatives and traditional leaders to encourage local community participation to deal with security as it affects them. PROSECs and DISECs forward their concerns and views to the ONS. It must be stressed that these committees are not intelligence-gathering agencies, nor is the ONS a security ministry; UK support to the end of 2006 was predicated on the principle that the ONS should not perform ministry functions. It is essentially a secretariat that alerts and informs the government and produces options, better honed by bringing the security sector constituents and other government departments together and merging their collective professional advice[4] for the NSC to decide upon. It then helps security sector constituents implement whatever the NSC directs.

During the post-colonial era, before war broke out in 1991, the army, the police and what remained of legal intelligence services were profoundly emasculated and reduced to heavily politicised institutions, often set against each other. The SLA and the SLP collapsed almost completely during the war: chains of command and lines of communication were broken; orders, pay and supplies rarely reached fighting troops or stations.

The inflated but broken SLA numbered around 16,000 at the height of the conflict. The new Republic of Sierra Leone Armed Forces (RSLAF) is now 10,300 strong, having taken in 2,600 former rebels and militiamen under the Military Reintegration Programme and downsized in three phases of military retirement (the Sierra Leone chief of defence staff called it 'rightsizing'[5]). The SLP is now approaching the national manpower target of 9,500, having been reduced severely by the ravages of war. The rationale for an RSLAF of 10,300 and an SLP force of 9,500 is not articulated formally; both force strengths need reviewing in depth.

Donor assistance to reform the armed forces is spearheaded by the UK-led IMATT, established formally in 2002 following the UK's military intervention. IMATT's mission is to support the GoSL in the development of effective, democratically accountable and affordable armed forces capable of meeting specified defence missions and tasks.[6] IMATT sums up its support as an 'effect',[7] which is the widespread, constant transfer of common themes, messages and practices to ensure an enduring transformation. At the end of 2006 IMATT employed just over 100 servicemen and included contributions from the UK, Canada, the United States, Nigeria and Jamaica. It is funded totally by the UK Africa Conflict Prevention Pool; its stakeholders are the UK Foreign and Commonwealth Office (FCO), Ministry of Defence (MoD), and the UK Department for International Development (DFID). The success of IMATT is dependent, however, upon two conditions. Firstly, IMATT credibility must be protected by providing objective and realistic advice, strictly managing expectations and acting as an exemplar; secondly, the RSLAF's ability and willingness to continue transformation must maintain momentum.[8]

The IMATT 'effect' is delivered by personnel deployed with the RSLAF, including brigades and battalions, the Armed Forces Training Centre, the Officers' Academy, the operational-level Joint Force Command Headquarters and the civilian-led MoD. Initially, IMATT held command and executive posts, but now only fills a handful of staff posts where specialist knowledge is required. IMATT personnel and two DFID-funded civilian posts in the MoD now act predominantly as advisers. IMATT's main effort is to help the RSLAF to 'think' rather than to give it 'things', and to engender an attitude that brings moral courage and integrity to the fore of decision-making at all levels. This emphasis is important in fostering strong local ownership and guarding against a dependency culture. But it is not always popular.

The SLP has received much technical and financial support from the UN, the Commonwealth and DFID. In contrast to the armed forces, this has been a 'top-down' approach, but with positive impacts, especially on improved higher management capacity. Unfortunately, insufficient attention has been given to policing reform at the lower tiers. This situation is expected to change as the DFID-sponsored Justice Sector Development Programme makes an impression out to 2010. Also, UN police regional advisory support teams deployed in 2006 are making their presence felt at the station level. In early 2007 the UN police in the provinces were reinforced by UK police working under UN direction. This UN force numbers less than 50 personnel (UN police strength in Sierra Leone has never exceeded 130). The SLP is unarmed (with the exception of the Operational Support Division – OSD) and relies on building relations with local communities for intelligence gathering. The fact that the SLP is an unarmed police service is unusual for Africa and reflects the GoSL's desire to gain the public's confidence.[9]

Security and Development (going around in circles)

The provision of basic security as a precondition for political, social and economic development (and well-being) is becoming increasingly recognised by practitioners and commentators.[10] The GoSL's PRSP underscored this emphasis by placing 'promoting good governance, peace and security' as Pillar One of its principles. Ideally, there should be a 'virtuous circle' of security: promotion of development, and then development sustaining security. For the security sector specifically, this means someone has to pay for the upkeep of the institutions within. Sierra Leone is not yet in a position to do so, and therefore the 'virtuous circle' is currently a 'vicious circle'. In 2006 DfID commissioned a report ('Security sector expenditure review' – SSER) to take stock and assess just how sustainable the state's security sector really is.[11] Put simply, the GoSL is unable to sustain, or indeed develop, the security sector without external assistance. If assistance were withdrawn, security may no longer be a given and vicious infighting could reappear. The GoSL has to build the 'virtue' of sustaining its own security and prevent sectoral infighting.

The SSER is sobering in its findings. Security is the highest single spending sector in Sierra Leone, representing 18.1 per cent (US$180 million) of the on-budget[12] total from 2003 to 2006 inclusive (the 2006 spend being forecast). Out of this security spend, 61 per cent went to the MoD/RSLAF and 24 per cent to the Ministry of Internal Affairs (MIA)/SLP. The vast majority of the spending was recurrent (operating costs); less than 1 per cent went towards sector development (capital expenditure). The ONS security sector review implementation plan of 2005[13] estimated non-recurrent spending requirements of US$69 million in 2006 to pursue modernisation, including adequate accommodation for the 42 per cent of the RSLAF who currently live in self-made shelters. This has not been forthcoming from the GoSL; the balance of development and capital investment has been provided off-budget through donor-executed assistance programmes.

In 2006 the security sector employed 33 per cent of the total number of public sector employees. Within the sector, 16.5 per cent are MoD/RSLAF; 14.2 per cent are MIA/SLP.

Public sector pay increases have not kept up with double-figure inflation; public servants on the lowest levels are earning less than US$1 per day. In sum, the GoSL is not able to deliver the services required in an affordable and sustained manner. As commander of IMATT and military adviser to the GoSL, this author said to the UK secretary of state for international development visiting Sierra Leone in July 2006, 'We are going to be right back where we started unless this is addressed with action, soon after the 2007 elections.'

Collaboration (more talking than walking)

While leading donors acknowledge the PRSP and are locked into various working groups with the GoSL, accounting for any donor programmes pursued by the host Ministry of Finance (MoF) is at best superficial. Off-budget support to the security sector does not enable full accounting of the true cost of security provision. Thus off-budget support undermines fiscal sustainability, as well as allocation and operational efficiency within the security sector and across government as a whole. The cost of in-kind support is not declared in many cases and is difficult to measure in others; some providers are reluctant to follow through or acknowledge the context. Egypt, for example, provided training for RSLAF air and ground crews in 2006, having made the one RSLAF helicopter fly briefly in 2005, without recognising that sustaining a serviceable transport helicopter is well beyond the RSLAF budget.

Collaboration between leading assistance agencies is also mixed. While DFID does not extend its development assistance to military capability, support for the creation of effective and accountable security and justice institutions is legitimate.[14] This has enabled DFID to fund directly the employment of civil advisers to the MoD, ONS and SLP, housing for the SLP and the RSLAF, severance payments to retired soldiers and policemen and contributions towards GoSL compensation payments to wounded soldiers and policemen and relatives of those killed in action. In addition, the UK Africa Conflict Prevention Pool (ACPP) can support military expenditure other than for weaponry and ammunition. The ACPP joint funding arrangement[15] is important, as it provides the foundation for a comprehensive, more holistic, approach to UK security sector support. It certainly promotes close UK FCO, MoD and DFID working relationships in-country.

In practical terms, the relationship with the World Bank is not as constructive. While policy may be aligned between the World Bank and DFID, interpretation of policy by World Bank agents in the Sierra Leone MoF often runs counter to SSR plans. The Sierra Leone deputy minister of defence expressed frustration when attempts to trade manpower for modernisation and infrastructure and greater financial accountability were countered by MoF officials. These officials cited World Bank rulings on what did or did not constitute a poverty reduction measure, which invariably blocked defence spending on anything other than the staples of wages, rice and fuel.

A Regional Approach (so far, rather slow)

ECOWAS was active throughout the 1990s in Sierra Leone, but intervened for the last time in 1998 before being relieved by the UN, and stepped into Liberia in 2003 while the UN assembled its force. Until 2004, when the African Union (AU) deployed troops, ECOWAS was the only regional organisation in Africa to use military forces in an attempt to manage a crisis. Not surprisingly, ECOWAS has been very receptive to the AU's standby force concept, under which the five regional economic communities in Africa will each introduce a military element to their structure and establish a regional stand-by military force for conflict prevention and management.

An ECOWAS standby force headquarters is being established in Nigeria under a Nigerian brigadier. Sierra Leone has a staff officer on that team.

The proposed ECOWAS force structure has Sierra Leone donating – or generating – at least an infantry company, possibly a battalion. The debate in 2006 was whether to select the company or battalion as a whole (based on the best operational evaluation reports) or to select the best individuals to make up the company/battalion. Either way, there was one major incentive to be noted: the possibility of being employed on UN subsistence rates was highly attractive. A small number of officers have already been employed as UN military observers (the SLP has also deployed individuals to be part of the UN Civilian Police Force – CIVPOL – in Haiti).

Regional involvement in Sierra Leone has been spearheaded by ECOWAS, and significant regional contributions have been made to UN forces in the country. The weakness of this involvement has been the lack of effective funding. The UN provided staple supplies to UNAMSIL troops, but there was little forthcoming to support SSR. ECOWAS plans, made prior to UNAMSIL, to reform the SLA came to nothing, again because there was no funding. A regional presence in UNAMSIL was not a conduit to external assistance from Nigeria (though RSLAF personnel are invited to attend the Nigerian Staff and War Colleges). In recognition of the efficiency and appropriateness of regional arrangements, IMATT funded individual training for the RSLAF in Ghana.

The three leading donors to the region – the United States (US), UK and France – actively support the ability of ECOWAS to prevent and manage conflict. The US is prepared to finance training and logistic support; the UK is financing preparations for AU operations (notably for Nigeria) and sponsoring the Kofi Annan International Peacekeeping Training Centre in Ghana. France supports training exercises; Canada, the European Union and the Netherlands have also offered to help develop ECOWAS capability to conduct peace support operations (including infrastructure for and staffing of the standby force headquarters in Nigeria). The US presence may become more significant with the creation of a new US military command called Africa Command (AFRICOM). An embryo of AFRICOM is already based in Germany, co-located with European Command (EUCOM). The AFRICOM concept includes basing headquarters on the African continent.[16]

Forward basing in West Africa would likely generate a greater US military presence in Liberia, which would imply a longer-term physical presence beyond training the new army. Interestingly, the concept also emphasises the need for greater collaboration between the US Department of Defense, the US Agency for International Development, partners and non-governmental organisations. The GoSL would welcome support from AFRICOM, but the ONS is wary that the US focus may be on countering terrorism, which is a low priority in Sierra Leone. (The main priorities for the ONS are issues of income generation and fighting crime.)

The poverty of the region brings pressures that obstruct investment in public goods, including the provision of security for the future. A tangible example is the ECOWAS proposal to build a logistic depot at Hastings airfield in Sierra Leone as part of the standby force capability. The US made available funds to construct and stock the depot, provided it would inherit the existing UN depot intact. However, when the GoSL handed the airfield to ECOWAS in November 2006, it had been stripped by the RSLAF (with GoSL approval). The project was no longer within the US budget. The proposal is now under review by the US and ECOWAS; Sierra Leone may no longer be the preferred location. This incident, which was a big disappointment to ECOWAS and donors, illustrates how lack of resources forces actors to live hand-to-mouth, to the detriment of longer-term investment. This is a culture that perpetuates the 'vicious circle' of an unsustainable security sector.

The emerging Africa Peace and Security Architecture, prompted by the New Partnership for Africa's Development (NEPAD) and launched in 2001, is immature and will not be self-sustaining for a long time; thus donors must continue to assist. The alternative would be essentially to let the establishment of the architecture fail altogether. Should that be the case, conflict will be more likely to emerge unchallenged and there would be no regional response. In West Africa's subregion, the Mano River Union (the presidents of Guinea, Sierra Leone and Liberia) met in February 2007 to discuss political and economic tensions in Guinea, and agreed that their state security organisations should share information.[17] However, while military-specific information exchange is occurring and Sierra Leone is playing a pivotal role, there are significant difficulties. The lack of established security architecture in Liberia frustrates Sierra Leone's ONS; there is no equivalent office in Guinea. Guinea itself looks like a failing state with an increasingly fragmented security sector.

National Security Sector Reform (within rather than without)

The RSLAF is being reformed from within; there is a new breed of officer class moving towards the top echelon. While the RSLAF and IMATT find the building of a training ethos to be a challenge, they are continuing annual training cycles to prepare troops for border duties and developing plans to provide troops for ECOWAS, AU or UN operations.

While the RSLAF achieved the 2003 Sierra Leone Defence Council target of reducing its numbers to 10,500 by the end of 2005 (almost a year ahead of schedule), further modernisation will require more manpower reductions to offset costs. A key consideration for the GoSL is how many more soldiers can be retired and successfully reintegrated into society. There was similar concern when the Civil Defence Force (CDF) was processed through the UN-administered disarmament, demobilisation and reintegration (DDR) programme and a smaller number accepted for the military reintegration programme (to be absorbed into the RSLAF). At the time, it was thought that CDF forces could find part-time employment in a territorial defence force to address potential threats from Liberia. While such part-time employment would have eased reintegration, once Liberia stabilised the idea was not pursued.

Thus all security services in Sierra Leone are full-time and formal, which is important for accountability. The chain of command is clear and there are no private armies. Possession of illegal weapons by former combatants is now monitored and under control. The CDF 'hunter-militia' legacy has withered away, to the extent that the death of CDF wartime leader Hinga Norman while on trial in Sierra Leone in 2007 occurred without violent reaction. Moreover, security structures are generally simple and transparent, which makes oversight more achievable and reduces the risk of public institutions becoming tools for private leverage.

By 2004 the security sector review was well under way. With DFID encouragement, the MoF decided to lead the way to accounting for the security sector as a whole by providing the sector with a budget ceiling. Thus allocations within the security sector would be decided by the NSC, in order to allow sector-wide prioritisation and encourage a focused, comprehensive and integrated budget. However, the inability to decide upon sector-wide priorities caused this approach to fail, and individual budget entities went back to bilateral discussions with the MoF.[18]

The 2005 ONS security sector review implementation plan offered another opportunity to transfer more administrative responsibility to the local security sector, ensuring a greater degree of accountability to donors. Having identified gaps, needs and priorities, the plan also represents a locally owned, accountable channel for management and coordination of funds. DFID is using this channel incrementally; in 2006 it put US$1.5 million at the disposal of the NSC Coordinating Group[19] to be spent according to the 2005 implementation plan. For the first time, sector entities, coordinated by the ONS, agreed among themselves on how the money should be spent. This is a good indication of how professional managers within the sector can work together for the greater good, but it has taken five years to achieve. However, it is still premature to resurrect the MoF's ambitions of 2004 and debate all security sector budgets as one at the far more politically oriented NSC.

Other process initiatives relating specifically to the RSLAF were the IMATT-inspired Plan 2010 and core review. The plan's objective was to deliver a smaller, better RSLAF with capable maritime and air wings. The RSLAF was to be self-sustaining, thus permitting the eventual withdrawal of IMATT. While the plan secured a funding profile from the UK ACPP for IMATT out to 2010, it was not so much owned as consented to by the Sierra Leone MoD and raised too many expectations. What the UK saw as an objective in the plan, the RSLAF saw as something to be provided by the UK. In addition, financial assumptions relating to the GoSL contribution were flawed, and the plan was deemed undeliverable.

The MoD then instigated a core review at the end of 2005. Based on the principles of sufficiency, efficiency, sustainability and quality over quantity, the review is ongoing and may well end up as a more comprehensive defence review under the new government. IMATT's insistence on local ownership of this review process may seem to be an impediment in the short term, but it will bring dividends in the longer term. In this regard, there are lessons to be learned from Plan 2010.[20]

The Leading Partner Model (not all it appears)

The UK is the major aid donor in Sierra Leone; Sierra Leoneans look to the UK as a past colonial master whose military intervention at the turn of this century helped save the country from an Armageddon scenario. DFID signed a memorandum of understanding with the GoSL in 2002, committing the UK to a ten-year partnership. IMATT is also expected to provide assistance until at least 2012.

The UK's lead in security sector assistance in Sierra Leone has brought breadth and depth to its reform. The sector lacks some specialist capabilities, particularly in the SLP, and needs modern equipment and better infrastructure. However, responsibilities are well understood and civil oversight seems to have taken root, particularly in the civilian-led, civilian and military staffed MoD. The ONS project, bringing apolitical coherence to the sector as a whole, is deemed a success. It has steadfastly refused to be anything less than neutral with regard to the major political parties and has been singularly objective in its pursuit of improved security. When the idea of a Ministry of Security began to circulate in 2006, both the ONS and the UK rebuffed it, considering it a dangerous politicisation of the sector.

Being the lead donor partner does not necessarily mean one's objectives go unchallenged, particularly over time, as the country's ruling elite no longer see their survival threatened by open conflict. The UK realises that DFID has limited leverage on the government to achieve the quick changes needed to facilitate effective governance and promote development. Furthermore, DFID has moved away from the standard model of policy conditionality to provide direct budget support in a single year, and aims to judge the impact annually.[21] Put differently, GoSL actions, not words, will trigger direct budget support. The fundamental governance dilemma in Sierra Leone is that good planning is profoundly difficult for its MoF: the ministry cannot predict what direct budget support it may receive. It also cannot judge whether DFID will consider actual results satisfactory enough for the release of tranches of funding. The same can be said for other ministries in receipt of assistance programmes.

However, being a major partner does provide a wider comprehension of the strengths and weaknesses of the host state and its machinery. This ought to enable more productive targeting of aid. There is also the opportunity to ensure that a greater amount of donor spending is made visible to the host government and taken into account within that government's overall fiscal strategy, and that the fiscal sustainability 'lens' is applied to decision-making.

National Capacity and Motivation (still immature)

UNAMSIL left Sierra Leone in December 2005, leaving only an integrated office behind, including a small team of military observers. Since then the Sierra Leone national apparatus has been solely responsible for security of the country. The SLP looks inwards to counter internal security threats and the RSLAF looks outwards to guard against external threats. This role clarity is enshrined in a recently revised 2006 NSC directive, 'Military Aid to the Civil Power', that tasks the SLP with primary jurisdiction on internal security issues.[22] The OSD element of the SLP, besides being trained to use small arms, is also prepared and equipped to control crowds, filling a role that would otherwise be performed by the military. This division of labour should resonate with the public: non-military civil security units are far more reassuring than armed soldiers with bayonets. While this subordination of military forces to the police in internal security situations is not the norm for an army in West Africa, the SLP and RSLAF have overcome their traditional rivalry; their relationship is much improved. In the past this rivalry was demonstrated by pulling political strings and making threats, but both security entities have begun to develop a common purpose – to perform their separate functions in order to establish a secure state.

Aside from the risks posed by Guinea, the first real 'stand-alone' test for Sierra Leone's security sector since peace was declared in 2002 came in August 2007 with the second presidential and parliamentary elections. Preparations were taken most seriously by the security sector, although logistic support was a constant challenge. The ONS, SLP and, when called upon briefly, the RSLAF remained apolitical and helped prevent serious disruption of the election process. A poignant metric of SSR success is that the ONS supported the National Election Commission's (NEC) lead on election planning and execution and accepted the secondary role of its sector. The NEC role of setting *policy* and the ONS role of performing *delivery* worked.

The Sierra Leone MoD was reorganised extensively in 2002; a civilian director general now sits alongside the chief of defence staff to advise the civilian deputy minister. Five years on, the ministry is beginning to feel competent and confident. Moreover, the role clarification provided by the 'Military Aid to the Civil Power' directive, in concert with the 2003 defence white paper, articulates the concept of SLP primacy in internal security. It has taken nearly five years of practice for this to be understood throughout the sector management and down to the SLP and RSLAF ranks. IMATT acted as a guardian of this process while SLP primacy took root.

Ownership of and involvement in change should not just be limited to the institutions most immediately affected. There is a requirement for involvement of various government departments as well as civil society to ensure that any changes are based on an accurate assessment of need, rather than just supply. The real success of the security sector review[23] in Sierra Leone was the level of consultation with the population. Since security is as much about perception as reality, if the people feel more secure through regular engagement with their government and if security sector institutions are demystified, people's perceptions of insecurity, and insecurity itself, are reduced. The more people feel they and their property are safe, the more likely they are to invest in the future in a bid for greater prosperity. Greater prosperity reduces the risk of conflict. It appears that Sierra Leone has learned this lesson: engage the people and, ultimately, perceptions of insecurity will decrease.

While the security sector architecture is maturing, putting that architecture to good use across the government is not. This is best demonstrated by the previous government's apparent reluctance to produce a national security policy.

Understanding the process of how sector budgets are determined is more important than absolute levels of expenditure.[24] In Sierra Leone, despite progress to date, there has been little enthusiasm at cabinet level for a national security policy that reviews the true needs and fiscal implications of ongoing security reform, and then allocates resources within the framework of a national budgetary process. Ministers have been preoccupied with operational matters and consider change a low priority in the medium to longer term. While the RSLAF may wish to modernise, it has little incentive when budgets are allocated arbitrarily and manpower, the largest financial commitment, is administered directly from the MoF. Discussions regarding the balance between manpower and living standards and equipment have unfortunately been absent at the cabinet level, despite concentrated ONS lobbying efforts.

This issue might change in the medium to longer term, as under the new APC government a minister of defence has been appointed. Under the previous government, the continuing appointment of the president as minister of defence was not conducive to a challenging, constructive cabinet debate about the security sector. Ministers assumed that Kabbah was content with the status quo, when actually it appeared that he was too remote to question it. (After elections in August 2007, a national security policy has been finalised and approved by the National Security Council.)

In essence, the government lacks the wider capacity to make better use of security sector progress to date. It sees the context as 'post-conflict', while the security sector now sees the context as 'fragile development'. A good example of the disconnect between the GoSL and its own institutions is the RSLAF proposal to establish a joint maritime authority (JMA) to exploit its maritime wing's capability to patrol national waters. While the objective of this proposal is to work with other ministries to prevent illegal fishing and impose fines upon offenders, the cabinet has consistently deferred making a decision on the JMA since 2004. Meanwhile, two ministers at the Department of Marine Resources have been reshuffled amid accusations of corruption. Such indecision and staff turmoil indicate that Sierra Leone, after five years of peace, does not have the indigenous capacity or motivation to continue security sector transformation without funding and direction provided by external assistance.

Lessons (following a straighter path)

Several practical lessons can be drawn from the above narrative of progress in Sierra Leone.

- Collaboration is vital. Covey et al. advocate that an intervention requires several mutually supporting coalitions: political, relief, military, rule of law, institution building, economic reconstruction and donor support.[25] Each coalition needs a leading nation or organisation. Their case study is post-1999 Kosovo, but the model can be applied to Sierra Leone. While good headway has been made, with the UK leading a smaller coalition embarked on military reform, more collaboration must be forthcoming on the security architecture as a whole. In particular, more collaboration is needed to support improved decision-making at the highest level and civil oversight, notably through developing constructive scrutiny by executive and legislative arms of government.
- A regional perspective must be taken. Retired UK Prime Minister Tony Blair summarised Sierra Leone's position well: 'Earlier this week I visited the people of Sierra Leone, still struggling, but at least able to contemplate a better future. But as important is the next-door state of Liberia, now properly democratic. It might never have been so, had Sierra Leone fallen into the hands of the gangsters.'[26]
- SSR takes time, is expensive and must be viewed more broadly than just as the reform of armed forces. A security sector is only truly reformed when it is self-motivating and contributing to its own transformation. There is no quick fix for organisational and institutional change. Until the 'virtuous circle' of security promoting development and development sustaining security is reached, an external donor has to fill the funding gap.
- If only the armed forces and police receive attention, as is often the case in SSR, it will prove more difficult to encourage civil oversight by defence or interior ministries at a later date. Producing better soldiers and policemen is fine, but unless they are placed under an uncomplicated and robust national security architecture that is accountable, affordable and sustainable, trouble will ensue. It should

be remembered that security sector institutions are government departments like any other; thus, where possible, reforms should be consistent and prioritised against efforts made in other ministries. Reform must include the finance ministry and the governance reform secretariat. The security sector does not stand in isolation; nor can external donors take responsibility for financing it indefinitely.

- SSR is a necessary focus for assistance, and must come before economic development can gather momentum. Once state and personal security is addressed, people need economic security. Society as a whole, not only the elite, must be part of the developing economy;[27] the public sector needs its share of economic growth to pay for essential services, including security.
- While the immediate priority may be SSR, economic reform must be undertaken concurrently and from the outset. Otherwise, there will be a time lag; the 'catch-up' time will be perilously fragile and will carry with it an increased risk of serious instability. A phased approach which looks at conflict management, reconstruction and development has limitations, because the linkages are much stronger than the sequential phases imply. The reluctance of DFID until 2005 to appoint a head of country office in Sierra Leone with appropriate authority significantly restrained assistance to economic development and is indicative of the limitations of the linear concept.
- A lead or framework partner model does have advantages, especially at the sector level. Moreover, if this lead can span several sectors, the approach will be more robust and sustainable. Reform of the RSLAF to date has prospered from this approach, in which the UK has led IMATT to provide a framework for other nations to 'lock' into. Similarly, DFID has led the wider reform of other elements across the sector, with emphasis upon the ONS and the SLP. The resulting continuity and coherence have been reassuring to the GoSL and provided the foundation for the developing security architecture. This model now needs to encompass the MoF and MIA. But above all, this framework partner approach is dependent on considerable political will at the highest levels of the lead donor nation.
- Local involvement is critical, in both design and implementation of reform. External pressure to change may facilitate progress in the short term, but this progress will not be sustainable unless those affected can see the benefits of change. Local ownership requires significant capacity-building and consumes more time than an externally driven quick-impact process. But it does ensure that the

foundations of change are stronger and able to survive leadership changes over time.

In Sierra Leone, great executive and legislative strides were taken in 2002–2003 that impacted heavily upon the security sector. Since then, despite lingering questions about the sustainability of Sierra Leone's reforms, the enthusiasm has been overtaken by a degree of complacency because the status quo is acceptable to the government,

Interestingly, Kotter has identified the first step in any transformation effort as the need to convince management that allowing a status quo to continue will be more dangerous than bringing about change.[28] Security sector players in Sierra Leone have long felt a sense of urgency, which the cabinet, until recently, has not. This touches upon the general issue that strong ownership at the sector level may conflict with weak ownership at the cabinet level. A survey[29] of perceptions carried out by the UK MoD in November 2006 found that concerns for the people of Sierra Leone were dominated by a lack of economic development. The sample also cited government as one of the factors inhibiting development progress.

This widespread discontent with the government, in conjunction with an increasingly improved civil/military relationship and perceptions of a more capable and powerful RSLAF, has the potential to create an unstable societal environment, possibly one in which the civilian population could encourage a coup. Given that the RSLAF displays an increasing tendency to position its civil/military relationship as a role rather than a code of conduct, a civilian population who start to see the military as a viable alternative to the government may coincide with an RSLAF receptive to the idea. Such a hypothesis points out the dangers of inconsistent levels of local ownership across government sectors.

Comparison and Conclusion (it all takes time)

In 2001 the SLA was effectively led by UK officers. While there were some courageous and capable SLA officers at battalion level and below, they were in the minority. UK officers were formally embedded in command positions, including that of the joint force commander. While the SLA was progressively being retrained by the UK, it was minimally equipped as marching infantry. Without UK spine, the SLA would have continued to fall into chaos and disrepute. Indeed, UNAMSIL's view at that time was that without international military assistance, complete disbanding of the SLA would have been the only option.

By 2006 the RSLAF had consolidated its formal role within the national security architecture. While trust is a rare commodity in Sierra Leone, particularly between the constituents of the security sector, the RSLAF showed due respect to its partners. It is now under civil control; its chain of command is in Sierra Leonean hands. While some corruption and patronage still exist, the RSLAF has improved its honesty, transparency and professional conduct more than most GoSL institutions. Most of the officers at battalion command level are competent and motivated, a training ethos is emerging and participation in AU and UN operations is close at hand.

However, battalion commanders are not confident enough of their standing to wish IMATT farewell yet. They still feel that without IMATT on hand to monitor standards, old habits in the chain of command might overwhelm their good deeds. The need to trade quantity for quality is recognised, but the RSLAF is frustrated by the lack of will and means to deliver such trade-offs on the part of other government departments. While they have an effective maritime wing, land mobility, communications and small-arms supplies, military infrastructure, especially housing, is pitiful. All that has been achieved to date remains fragile, and the risk of being undermined by a financial crisis is high. Without a fundamental review by the new government, the prediction of IMATT and the Sierra Leone MoD that the RSLAF by 2009 will only be able to sit, quite literally, in barracks and do nothing else may prove to be true. It is a dangerous state of affairs.

To quote Prime Minister Tony Blair again: 'The international action of the past few years hasn't transformed Africa; but it has undoubtedly made it better.'[30] This is true for Sierra Leone. For the UK military, making a difference in Africa means a long-term involvement, taking a regional perspective, being realistic about what is achievable and affordable, managing expectations tightly and working towards local ownership while being cognisant of national and regional politics.

When acting as a 'force for good', military assistance is never likely to be short term. Making a genuine difference in the development of conflict-ridden countries, turning them into productive, peaceful states, can be seen as a series of battles fought not on the field but within and among institutions. These battles may be won, lost or drawn, but they are worthwhile, in the light of the greater goals of peace, security and long-term economic stability.

Notes

1 The term 'security sector' includes the police, the military, the intelligence agencies, the prison services, other official security organisations and the civilian authorities that are meant to control and oversee these bodies. Department for International Development (2006) *Understanding and Supporting Security Sector Reform*, London: DFID, p. 7.

2 See www.daco-sl.org/encyclopedia/1_gov/1_4ons_progress_rpt.pdf (accessed 20 June 2007).

3 See www.daco-sl.org/encyclopedia/1_gov/prsp.htm (accessed 11 July 2007).

4 Diplomacy, information, security, economy and community are the headings that the ONS imposes upon its papers to the NSC.

5 Sierra Leone chief of defence staff, MoD press conference, 12 December 2005.

6 See www.statehouse-sl.org/policies/defence-white-paper.html (accessed 20 June 2007).

7 Commander IMATT (SL) (2006) *Directive for 2006*, January, Freetown: HQ IMATT (SL), p. 1.

8 Ibid., p. 2.

9 Albrecht, P. and Malan, M. (2006) *Post-Conflict Peacebuilding and National Ownership: Meeting the Challenges of Sierra Leone*, Berlin: Zentrum fur Internationale Friedenseinsatze, p. 131.

10 Schwarz, R. (2005) 'Post-conflict peace building: The challenges of security, welfare and representation', *Security Dialogue,* 36(4): 429–446.

11 Middlebrook, P. and Miller, S. (2006) 'Sierra Leone security sector expenditure review', commissioned by DFID Sierra Leone Country Office, September, pp. 1–3.

12 'On-budget' is income/expenditure declared in the government of Sierra Leone accounts. 'Off-budget' is not declared.

13 See www.daco-sl.org/encyclopedia/1_gov/1_4ons.htm (accessed 11 July 2007).

14 UK House of Commons, International Development Committee (2006) 'Conflict development: Peacebuilding and post-conflict reconstruction, international development – First special report 2006', HC 923-I, 19 December, p. 71.

15 Sierra Leone accounted for £107 million of the total ACPP spend 2001–2005. Department for International Development (2006) *Reducing Conflict in Africa: Progress and Challenges*, Africa Conflict Prevention Pool Performance Report, 2001–2005, September, London: DFID, p. 8.

16 See www.eucom.mil/africom (accessed 20 June 2007).

17 UN Secretary-General (2007) 'Fourteenth progress report of the Secretary-General on UNMIL to the UN Security Council', UN Doc. 5/2007/151, 15 March, p 3.

18 Middlebrook and Miller, note 11 above, p. 3.

19 The Coordinating Group is the body of public servants (department director general level) which guides the routine work of the ONS, and its interaction with other government departments, on behalf of the NSC.

20 The lessons of Plan 2010 were that local engagement is not enough, ownership is required; and that expectation management is of key importance – both host and donor should be open as to what their responsibilities are and committed to meeting them.

21 UK House of Commons, International Development Committee, note 14 above, p. 41.

22 See www.daco-sl.org/encyclopedia/1_gov/1_4ons/macp.htm (accessed 11 July 2007).

23 See www.daco-sl.org/encyclopedia/1_gov/1_4ons_progress_rpt.pdf (accessed 20 June 2007).

[24] Hendrikson, D. and Ball, N. (2002) 'Off-budget military expenditure and revenue: Issues and policy perspectives for donors', Occasional Papers 1, January, Conflict, Security and Development Group, King's College, London, pp. 1, 10.

[25] Covey, J., Dziedzic, J. and Hawley, L. (2005) *The Quest for Viable Peace: International Intervention and Strategies for Conflict Termination*, Washington, DC: US Institute of Peace Press.

[26] Blair, T. (2007) 'What I've learned', *The Economist*, 2 June.

[27] Covey et al., note 25 above, p. 208.

[28] Kotter, J. (1995) 'Leading change: Why transformation efforts fail', *Harvard Business Review*, 4231: 60.

[29] The description of this survey is based upon the author's immediate debrief of the survey team in his capacity as commander of IMATT (SL). The hypothesis was raised by the team and supported by the author.

[30] Blair, T. (2007) 'Speech in South Africa', *Prime Minister's Speeches*, available at www.pm.gov.uk (accessed 1 June 2007).

Chapter 4

Operation Pebu and the Ministry of Defence

Aldo Gaeta

Introduction

This chapter documents the history of Operation Pebu between April 2003 and March 2006. It is an overview of the progress and development of the project, and does not attempt to document every change in contract between the government of Sierra Leone (GoSL) and its contractors, nor those relating to contracts let by the UK Department for International Development (DFID). The focus of the narrative is the construction of accommodation for soldiers of the Republic of Sierra Leone Armed Forces (RSLAF) and their families, with which Operation Pebu has become synonymous.

Background

Following the end of the civil war, there was a need to restructure the RSLAF in preparation for its assumption of national security responsibilities once the UN Mission in Sierra Leone (UNAMSIL) terminated. This restructuring included the need to consolidate and reduce RSLAF locations outside Freetown, from over 50 headquarters (HQ)/company/platoon sites to nine battalion barracks and three brigade HQs. Restructuring and development plans recognised the need to construct new accommodation for the RSLAF or, where possible, to refurbish existing accommodation.

Initial cost estimates for the development of suitable infrastructure were in excess of $200 million. Since it was expected that most of the required funding would be forthcoming from the international community (given the magnitude of the amount required), there was no attempt by the GoSL to build this project into its own expenditure plans. However, after being tabled at a 2002 donors' conference in Paris, the project's bid for international assistance was rejected. Given the importance of infrastructure redevelopment, meetings were held involving the RSLAF, the Ministry of Defence and the International Military Assistance Training Team (IMATT) to consider how to proceed. Operation Pebu (*pebu* means 'shelter' in the Mende language) was conceived at these meetings.

The intent of Operation Pebu was to facilitate better control, direction and maintenance of RSLAF units and improve the morale and welfare of soldiers and their dependants by providing a better standard of living accommodation. Its concept was to establish and implement a development plan that will deliver new or refurbished barracks, built to an interim standard, in order to put in place the infrastructure necessary to allow the development and implementation of a formation training cycle by May 2004.

Aim

The project foresaw the refurbishment of an existing brigade HQ and barracks (in Teko) and the building of seven battalion barracks for soldiers and their families and two brigade HQs on greenfield sites. Battalion barracks were to be built (after some debate and negotiation with paramount chiefs) at Simbakoro, Moyamba, Yele, Kambia, Kabala, Pujehun and Kailahun. Brigade HQs would be located at Kenema and Bo. (The brigade HQ at Kenema was not part of the original plan, but was added in June 2003 when a request for additional support was submitted.)

Each battalion site would have technical infrastructure (offices and stores) and family quarters. The brigade HQs would have similar technical infrastructure. All sites would have wells and deep-trench latrines.

The battalion sites were to be self-build projects, using soldiers as construction workers, while the brigade HQs were to be built by contractors. Work began in February/March 2003, and was (ambitiously) scheduled to be completed by May/June 2004.

Funding

Because the GoSL could not finance the entire cost of Operation Pebu, DFID was approached through IMATT for assistance. Initial funding was set at £3m in January/February 2003, with DFID contributing £1.9m and the GoSL £1.1m. A formal exchange of letters was signed by the British High Commission and the GoSL in May 2003. Although some of the funding was used to pay the contractors building the brigade HQs, most of it was scheduled to be spent on materials and rudimentary tools, since construction on greenfield sites was to be carried out by RSLAF personnel. Supervision of the project was the responsibility of IMATT personnel.

By June 2003 changes in the initial design of the family accommodation (discussed below) required additional funding. The GoSL (through the deputy defence minister and His Excellency President Kabbah) approached DFID for this support. Additional funding was forthcoming; DFID would supply another £1.7m and the GoSL another £0.9m. This additional money was pledged without a formal investment appraisal.

DFID funds were expended both locally and through an international procurement contract. Funding provided by the GoSL was spent locally on materials procurement. Between 2003 and 2004, rapid inflation in Sierra Leone had a major impact on available funding.

Because there were several elements to the project, it was a relatively straightforward process, at least in the early stages, to allocate financial responsibility for discrete elements to either the GoSL or DFID. However, with the upgraded barrack design, this became more difficult because the GoSL could not afford the changes on all three sites it was initially allocated. By June 2003 responsibility for development of the Simbakoro greenfield site was split between the GoSL and DFID, causing management difficulties, particularly in relation to materials procurement.

Design

The original design for barracks accommodation was a one-room mud-brick construction, a decision made on the assumption that this housing was a three- to five-year temporary measure. However, within a few months of initial funding, concerns were raised within the GoSL and RSLAF about accommodation standards – for example, rudimentary sanitation facilities, lack of a 'chop house' and overall lack of space. (It is likely that there was some political pressure applied at this juncture, since opponents of Kabbah's government were voicing concerns over the accommodation standards.)

There is little existing documentary evidence to reveal decisions made at that time or what the catalyst was, but by June 2003 the initial design for a family home evolved into a three-room structure with veranda, using Hydraform block technology (the Hydraform process is discussed below). No written evidence exists to indicate that any re-evaluation of the timeframe for completion of the project occurred. It is also clear that these changes were not factored into any work schedule; project timelines were not extended.

Project Management

Project management of Operation Pebu was, with the benefit of hindsight, not well planned. Although it was jointly funded, Operation Pebu was a GoSL-owned project. The project director was the RSLAF joint support commander[1] (JSC); the project manager was an RSLAF lieutenant colonel. It should be noted that at the start of the project the post of JSC was being filled by an IMATT officer, pending the appointment of a suitable RSLAF officer. This, however, did not make Operation Pebu an IMATT project, since all IMATT officers were on loan service to the RSLAF. The regular rotation of IMATT personnel (generally yearly, or on a six-month basis) caused significant problems for the management and development of Operation Pebu – which, by any standards, was a complex project.

IMATT engineers, embedded within the RSLAF Engineer Regiment (the CO Engineer Regiment post was filled by an IMATT officer), both supervised and advised the construction process. DFID had a very limited technical presence in Freetown, and thus did not provide dedicated engineering support to Operation Pebu. (DFID did not have a country office in Sierra Leone at the time, but a small administrative set-up with authority for policy and funding vested in DFID's West Africa Department in London.) DFID's main link to Operation Pebu was through the DFID-funded civil and financial advisers in the Ministry of Defence (MoD), who tried to keep a handle on the complex financial arrangements. By default, these posts came to represent the DFID presence on the ground, although it could be argued that because of their primary duties, neither could devote the necessary time to Operation Pebu.

An Operation Pebu steering committee was formed under the leadership of the JSC; it met for the first time in early May 2003. From this, an 'integrated project team' emerged which would deal with the practical aspects of Pebu, taking its direction from the steering committee, and an 'Operation Pebu cell' created within the joint force HQ. It is worth noting here that – despite advice from UK advisers – there was no senior or significant involvement from the MoD in Operation Pebu committees. This lack of senior management 'buy-in' was responsible for the lack of commitment and control witnessed throughout the project, but notably in the early stages.

Construction

While the refurbishment of Teko and the construction of the brigade HQs were carried out by local construction companies, the bulk of the building work (i.e. the development of the greenfield sites) was to be performed by soldiers as labourers – which, ideologically, appeared to have benefits.

The basic mud-block building required no construction training, but some artisan skills were required for tasks such as carpentry. IMATT used its own development funds to train a number of artisans within the RSLAF infantry battalions.

There was, however, a flaw in this plan to self-build. While the CO of the Engineer Regiment had a major responsibility for the development of the project, he did not have responsibility for the manpower – this remained with COs of the individual battalions. Thus responsibility for productivity was vested in an individual who had no defined role in the project. Consequently, it was not possible to know in advance how many labourers would actually be available at any one time. This flaw was particularly significant when the production method changed to Hydraform blocks.

Other drawbacks of the self-build scheme emerged as the project progressed, including soldiers' training and morale issues. The adverse effect on morale was further exacerbated when it became known that, through a DFID-funded programme, accommodation for the Sierra Leone Police (SLP) was being built commercially and to a much higher standard than that of Operation Pebu.

Hydraform

With the proposal to change the design of the barrack accommodation in June 2003, a plan was put forward to change the construction method from mud blocks to Hydraform blocks. This change was included in the submission for additional funding at that time.

Although, on paper, changing to this technology appeared to offer some positive benefits that would aid the construction process, it is fair to say that it was one of the most disastrous decisions made during the lifetime of Operation Pebu.

To the best of anyone's knowledge, Hydraform blocks had never been used on a major construction project in Sierra Leone. The decision to purchase Hydraform machines was based on an advertisement in the back of a local magazine. No trials of the machines ever took place, nor did anyone visit South Africa (where they are produced) to carry out a proper appraisal of Hydraform's applicability to Operation Pebu.

In brief, using soil and cement, this technology uses machines to produce construction blocks. In theory, the machines produce blocks more quickly and in a more consistent form than a manual process. This, however, is only one part of the process. The soil has to be of the right type, which is not generally found in West Africa (a fact that only came to light a year after the first machines were purchased for Operation Pebu). Moreover, the blocks also had to undergo a strict curing process.

Although mixing the soil and cement was a mechanical process, there was still a labour-intensive element to the work. The soil had to be dug out and transported manually, by wheelbarrows, headpans and jerrycans, to the production site. The construction team had no access to any form of mechanical transport, such as diggers, dumpers or lorries, to aid this process.

Hydraform machines are technically sophisticated; machine down-time through breakdowns, some of which could be attributed to poor maintenance of the machines by RSLAF personnel on site, decreased the rate of block production. To deal with this problem, personnel from the Engineer Regiment were tasked with the maintenance of the machines, but were largely ineffective because of lack of fuel and transport to the sites where the machines were located.

Six Hydraform machines were purchased from additional funding approved in July 2003; another nine were purchased in February 2004 in an effort to speed up married quarters construction. Despite the assurance in Hydraform's advertising that they were capable of producing 1,500 blocks per day 'under factory conditions', the machines used on Operation Pebu never produced more than a maximum of around 800 per day. Even at that rate of production, many of the blocks were unusable because of problems with the soil and poor curing procedures. (The curing process required significant quantities of water, which was not always available at some sites with non-functioning wells.)

Procurement

The procurement of materials caused further problems. DFID specified at the time of the agreement that all its funds had to be used in accordance with its procurement processes. In essence this meant using the International Procurement Agency for purchasing materials. This caused some resentment within the higher echelons of the RSLAF and MoD. There was a widely held view that, given DFID's role in international development, the GoSL should have been allowed to use its funds to support smaller local businesses.

In order to control the materials once they arrived in-country, DFID engaged the services of a local civil engineering company, which allocated personnel to each 'DFID' site. The civil engineers' role was to receive and issue the material required for construction. However, it became clear later that some personnel did not perform effectively, often allowing themselves to be pressurised by military personnel on site, who acquired material for personal purposes. Since there were no established audit requirements, there was very little control over materials once they arrived in-country.

GoSL procurement of materials was effected through a limited tender exercise carried out by the Central Tender Board.[2] This brought with it other problems, including severe delays in issuing tender documents and awarding contracts. Some contracts were paid 100 per cent up front; in some cases, material turned up on site significantly in advance of need. In the case of cement, this lack of project organisation was particularly wasteful, with hundreds of bags deteriorating because they could not be stored under proper conditions.

The GoSL procurement process for Operation Pebu materials received significant attention from the Anti-Corruption Commission because of allegations of corrupt practices in awarding contracts. Although nothing was ever proven, the Pebu tendering process appeared to be restricted to a limited number of contractors, all of which quoted much higher prices than those being paid for similar goods by DFID for other projects. Rapid in-country inflation during 2003/2004 also had a major impact on procurement, with commodities such as cement costing significantly more in 2004 than in 2003.

Progress

In all probability, the initial planning timeframe was entirely unrealistic. For example, before construction of family and technical accommodation could begin, the seven greenfield sites had to be completely cleared and prepared. The initial planning did not take into account the difficulties and delays in procuring construction material on this scale in a country with very poor road infrastructure, nor the lack of mechanical transport available to the project. There was also a naïve view that RSLAF soldiers would be enthusiastic about spending their military time performing manual labour.

In early 2003 initial funding was based on a simple mud-block design. By the time the request for additional funding for the upgraded married quarters design was submitted in June 2003, little construction had taken place. Further delays occurred during the introduction of the Hydraform machines and their initial use. Lack of engagement by senior MoD personnel adversely impacted on progress.

Early in 2004, following a change of IMATT personnel, engineers visited the Operation Pebu greenfield sites and conducted an in-depth progress analysis. The stark conclusion was that it was unrealistic to expect more than 12 per cent of soldiers' married quarters to be completed on the greenfield sites by the onset of the 2004 rainy season. (The original plan for Operation Pebu had envisaged 100 per cent completion by this time.[3]) Based on a mathematical calculation of the number of blocks required per site in relation to production actually achieved, it would take at least another six years to complete the project.

This assessment led to the procurement of the additional nine Hydraform block-making machines in February 2004 in an effort to increase production. Although the extra machines increased the number of blocks produced, they did not have the expected impact for various reasons, including the intensely manual nature of the process, outlined above, and ineffective equipment care procedures. In addition, the realisation that the building project would not deliver houses for the soldiers and their families within the planned timeframe was a source of motivational problems. Although the original concept of the Operation Pebu project was put forward as a morale booster for the army, the reality of the tedious and arduous block-making process did little to encourage enthusiasm.

In keeping with the RSLAF ownership concept of Operation Pebu, both the project director and project manager were RSLAF officers. Block-making and construction of the dwellings were the responsibility of individual infantry battalion COs on the sites. The differing rates of progress on each site, caused in some instances by inefficient use of resources or insufficient deployment of personnel, could be attributed to some extent to the management and supervision skills of the individual COs.

In May 2004, following much discussion with various parties in Freetown, the commander of IMATT and the senior UK civil adviser to the MoD approached DFID for additional funding. This time, however, the request was put forward with several well-considered options to accelerate project progress, the favoured one being the removal of the block-making task from the RSLAF and transferring it to IMATT (using local labour), with an estimated cost of some £3.8m. This request was rejected by DFID, which was now concerned at the spectacular lack of achievement to date. Instead, DFID instructed an independent review of Operation Pebu by a team from Levitt Bernstein, an international housing consulting firm. It should be noted that all contractor-built elements of the project were either completed or near to completion by this point.

What Happened Next?

The Levitt Bernstein visit to Sierra Leone took place in August 2004, but prior to this, having accepted that there would be no additional funding for Operation Pebu, IMATT, RSLAF and local DFID personnel began to consider more radical options to achieve project progress, given that no single battalion site had more than 10–12 per cent of quarters constructed. The option proposed at a meeting chaired by the deputy defence minister was to concentrate efforts and material on the two sites deemed to be of most strategic importance because of their proximity to the border areas – Kailahun and Pujehun. There was no proposal that considered what would happen after completion of these sites, because nobody could predict what materials would still be available or what the chances of additional funding would be. At this time it was evident that, because of waste, loss of materials and the effects of inflation, original funding would not be enough to complete the entire project. The proposal to concentrate on the two border sites was accepted and all efforts of the Operation Pebu project team were focused on completing them by the end of 2005. This involved not only the logistical challenge of moving material to the two sites, but also structural changes in project management affecting both IMATT and the Engineer Regiment, which would have control of the labour force.

The Levitt Bernstein report, produced in late August/early September, was, not surprisingly, highly critical of the project, stating that essentially it was ill-defined, poorly managed and there was a danger that 'it could result in the creation of new slums'. Although it was a damning assessment of what had happened, the report made little attempt to suggest any sensible way forward, except to recommend that construction should be procured commercially. (Subsequent costing suggested that this could amount to £10.5m per site.)

From late 2004 to early 2006 work progressed on both sites, but again the planned timescale for completion was not achieved. During 2005 two significant events happened. First, the demarcation that had existed between GoSL and DFID funding was removed, allowing all funds to be pooled for the benefit of the project; second, the head of DFID (a country office was established in early 2005) wrote to the deputy defence minister releasing the remainder of DFID funds to the project. At this stage, all parties were advised that no further funding would become available for Operation Pebu. By the end of 2005 the sites at Kailahun and Pujehun were still incomplete.[4]

Conclusion

Where did Operation Pebu go wrong? There is no easy answer to this question. The project failed on so many counts that it is best described as conceptually flawed.

Although there were some successes, notably in the contractor-built elements of the project (i.e. brigade HQs, wells and latrines), Operation Pebu is synonymous with the construction of family accommodation on seven greenfield sites to house the restructured RSLAF outside Freetown. The sheer scale of the project was never really considered. Taking into account soldiers and their family members, the estimated population to be housed would be in excess of 2,500 per site. In addition, it was perhaps over-ambitious to plan to carry out simultaneous construction on seven remote greenfield sites in a country where roads and communications infrastructure are very basic or, in some cases, non-existent. To think it possible to achieve 100 per cent completion within one year (bearing in mind that Sierra Leone has a five-month rainy season) using soldiers to carry out the bulk of construction defies explanation.

No single organisation is completely to blame. Operation Pebu was jointly funded by DFID and the GoSL, with DFID providing the greater part of the funds and the GoSL 'owning' the project. In addition, IMATT played a significant part in its management and supervision. There was no project manager, which would be unthinkable in a project of this magnitude in the developed world. DFID funding was decided in a random fashion; there was no attempt to construct a project strategy. IMATT personnel rotated frequently and its internal structure changed during the life of Operation Pebu, based on issues unrelated to the project. Finally, while the project was owned by the GoSL, there was no technical expertise within the RSLAF to lead such an undertaking.

The procurement of materials was badly handled by both sides. Although DFID procedures were largely effective in getting the materials into the country and on site, local arrangements for receipt and issue were less than satisfactory.

The decision to switch to Hydraform block-making was based on nothing more than an advert. It is difficult to believe that any major project in the developed world would incorporate new and untested technology across a major project when that project was already showing signs of delay.

Although the original house design changed, no attempt was made to reassess project timelines in light of those changes.

No senior personnel in the MoD ever actively engaged with Operation Pebu. Given the problems encountered with obtaining local resources (for example, transport, fuel and rice) and the lack of motivation within all ranks of the RSLAF, involvement by personnel who could influence these areas would likely have been beneficial.

There were motivational and morale issues affecting the soldiers. Operation Pebu was sold as a project that would be completed within one year. Even though it was obvious that the project was drifting, the expectations of soldiers and their families were not well managed. From a military training perspective, it appears to be unwise to take soldiers away from their military work and assign them to manual labour.

The realisation that the SLP was provided with contractor-built accommodation (paid for by DFID) constructed to a higher standard than Operation Pebu had a significant effect on RSLAF motivation and morale.

Finally, each battalion site was envisaged as a small town; however, there were no family/quality of life enhancements (e.g. proper sanitation, schools, churches, mosques or markets) incorporated into the design.

Notes

1. Following a restructuring of the RSLAF in 2004, the role of the JSC was subsumed by the joint force commander and, accordingly, the JFC became the project director.
2. The Central Tender Board was the main body responsible for letting contracts that were in excess of a certain value. This organisation was effectively disbanded in 2005 when the new procurement legislation came into being.
3. Accordingly, the start date of the new joint force cycle was set as June 2004. This cycle, designed to give structure and focus to infantry battalion life and to provide opportunities for real capacity-building, foresaw rifle companies rotating between training (where targets would have to be achieved), operations (support to police land border patrols) and regimental life. Each would be for four to five months.
4. They were completed in early 2008.

Chapter 5

The Security-Development Nexus in Sierra Leone

Mark White

Introduction

This chapter does not focus on the individual successes within the Sierra Leonean security sector itself over the duration of the security sector reform (SSR) process. Instead, it considers the interconnections and disjuncture between security and development that occurred during my time in Sierra Leone. The chapter attempts to demonstrate that while significant progress has been made since 1999 in ensuring that security and development are *interrelated*, there is still some way to go before they are fully *integrated* into either policy or programmatic practice.

Had security and development been better integrated at the outset of UK intervention, more progress would have been made on the core development agenda in Sierra Leone than there has been to date. This is my personal view and may seem excessively critical – an unfortunate legacy, perhaps, of being too close to the issues.

While I believe that SSR undertaken in Sierra Leone still sets the benchmark for success in the field of SSR programming, there are some valuable lessons that can be learnt. This is the case both within the sector itself and for the interrelationship between security and the broader development agenda.

The Security and Development See-Saw

In post-conflict environments, security and development are sometimes described as two sides of the same coin. This should not be the case. Instead, they could be seen as a see-saw. At some stages, support for one might outweigh support for the other, but wherever possible they should be in equilibrium. This requires a careful balancing act by both the international community and the host government. At any stage, overloading one could cause other fragile entities to collapse. For individuals responsible for making these decisions, it is rather akin to walking a tightrope with no safety net underneath.

In a highly political decision-making environment, it is almost inevitable that excessive caution is exercised by both governments and donors. People would rather not make a decision than make the wrong one, which is why so often the status quo is maintained. Furthermore, as the various reform actors move away from the immediate post-conflict period, it becomes even more difficult to overcome this reluctance to be held accountable. But as post-conflict countries progress along the conflict spectrum, there is an increasing need to ensure that security and development issues are placed on the same page, rather than destined to be opposites that never intertwine. It is only then that the trade-offs, synergies and challenges between security and development can be understood and debated.

These discussions and debates are, by their very nature, difficult, particularly in a resource-constrained environment: one cannot please all actors in a given reform process all of the time. However, without these discussions we are left with a series of rather glib assertions, such as 'development needs security and security needs development'.

What Sierra Leone experienced between 2005 and 2007 was a failure to merge security and development into an integrated relationship. Rather than use the poverty reduction strategy paper (PRSP) process as a springboard to integration, the government of Sierra Leone (GoSL) used the safety and stability created through effective SSR to rest on its laurels. The international community were equally unprepared for the 'post-post conflict period' and struggled to demonstrate a peace dividend to a frustrated population. Ironically, at times this resulted in the international community bearing more responsibility for maintaining a fragile peace than the democratically elected government. In short, there was security but there was no development, and while it was true to say that security now required development, no one was sure how best to achieve this.

The UK Department for International Development and the Security and Development Agenda

Security and development are clearly linked, but it has taken development agencies a long time to articulate in their policies and mission statements why this is so. This is in part due to the conceptual difficulties many development professionals have in engaging with the security sector, as well as a shortage of relevant capacity and experience within these agencies. Effective SSR facilitation requires a coherent 'whole-of-government approach' and few donor governments have the coordinating architecture or the political will to engage in what is seen by many as an all too difficult agenda.

DFID is more advanced in this area than some other bilateral donor agencies. Having broadened its engagement with the 'traditional' national security agenda, it has developed an approach that sees security as a basic public service – akin to health, education, street lighting and refuse collection – provided by a government accountable to its population. Both the delivery of security and the expectation among populations that governments will indeed deliver security to their citizens are regarded as key first steps in the development of social contracts between states and citizens. The provision of security is equally regarded as laying the foundation for broader accountability mechanisms in other sectors. There remains a clear gap between policy and practice, however, as evidenced by the fact that a significant proportion of the population in sub-Saharan Africa receives security and justice services from non-state actors. Nonetheless, the challenge of seeing security as a public good at the policy level has been won in development circles, for the time being at least.

Security and Development in Sierra Leone

It was the belief in the above principles that prompted DFID to embark on what was seen as a very non-traditional development programme in Sierra Leone at the end of 2002. It started with an unusual decision made by then UK Secretary of State for International Development Clare Short to agree a ten-year memorandum of understanding (MoU) between the UK government and the GoSL that binds both parties to a series of commitments until 2012. This type of arrangement was unique at the time and was a consequence of UK national and developmental interests aligning. Furthermore, it was coupled with a broader geopolitical commitment to demonstrate that a consolidated defence, diplomatic and development effort, as evidenced by the Global and Africa Conflict Prevention Pools, could deliver a stability sum total in excess of its constituent departmental parts. In other words, pooling the human and financial resources of the Foreign and Commonwealth Office (FCO), the Ministry of Defence (MoD) and DFID

harder it is to justify spending large sums of money on conflict prevention. Unfortunately, rather than consolidating success, in 2005 when the PRSP process was being finalised, Sierra Leone was ceding priority to other countries, such as the Democratic Republic of Congo, Sudan and Liberia next door.

Security, Development and the International Donor Community – A Strategic Deficit?

When PRSP commitments were being considered, the main issue was how to continue support to the security sector and consolidate successes while allowing the development space to be maximised – and all with the same amount of available money. Not easy. This would not have been as big a problem as it was had the international community been better coordinated. If all donors had collectively agreed with the government as to where Sierra Leone was situated on the post-conflict spectrum and aligned their development programmes accordingly, it would have been possible for donor agencies to divide the work based on comparative advantage. However, in 2005 there were very few donors active in the country; there was certainly no agreement on Sierra Leone's post-conflict trajectory. Some donors were still engaged in humanitarian operations, while others were focused on traditional development programmes. In an environment where there were few external actors, it was vital that the international community cooperated, rather than competed.

Although this might seem counterintuitive – fewer donors should mean coordination is easier – there were two reasons why this was not the case. First, fewer donors meant more competition for power and leadership, because no donor wanted to accept a supporting role. Thus whereas in other countries there are clear divisions between small but flexible donors and behemoths, everyone in Sierra Leone views themselves as important. Second, the biggest issue has been the competition between bilateral and multilateral donors. The UN, European Commission and World Bank are not accustomed to working in a country in which a bilateral has more political access and spending muscle than a multilateral. It took time for the multilaterals to respond positively to such a challenge.

Finally, there were inconsistent messages delivered to the government on its spending allocations. The GoSL was asking the international community to provide larger sums of money in support of programmes aimed at economic growth and increasing tax revenue. However, in order to do so, Sierra Leone was required to take up the slack caused by the reallocation of resources away from sectors that had previously been primarily supported by external funding. These fiscal decisions were made harder by the International Monetary Fund's insistence that the GoSL should increase the proportion of its spending on health and education, meaning that certain sectors would move from receiving significant to limited support within a relatively short time frame.

There are clear lessons of sustainability that need to be learnt from the Sierra Leonean experience. In 2006, when I left Sierra Leone, the SLP needed to replace 100 vehicles a year of its 800-strong fleet; it could afford to replace only ten. (The only thing worse than not having any capacity is having temporary capacity that is then taken away.) Additionally, there are urgent lessons that need to be learnt at the strategic level regarding planning capacity for post-post-conflict environments, before history repeats itself in other SSR interventions. I believe that the UN could play an extremely important strategic coordination role here, working rather than competing with strong bilateral partners. In many of these environments the UN has the people but limited funding; the bilaterals have the money but few people. There is clearly an alliance that can be forged here to mutual benefit. Such alliances should not be allowed to be dependent on personality rather than process.

Security and Development post-PRSP – Prioritisation and Costing

When the final PRSP was published in the spring of 2005, the security sector had managed to convince its political masters of the NSSR's strategic position within it. The sector can therefore be found under Pillar One of the PRSP: 'promoting good governance, peace and security'. In May 2005 the NSSR was launched by the president; he noted the links between the NSSR and the PRSP in his inaugural speech. The security sector, buoyed by this support from the highest level, began to develop activities to support the recommendations identified in the NSSR, in the hope of persuading the international community to provide implementation funding.

However, the recommendations needed to be adapted slightly in the light of the new links with the PRSP. There was also a need for a multi-stakeholder approach to solve challenges identified at both national and regional levels. It was clear at the outset that the costs of delivering against NSSR recommendations would be huge; hence, careful prioritisation was required to ensure both the realism of stakeholder funding and the contribution to poverty reduction. Activities were ranked on a scale from 1 to 5 on the basis of the ability of the activity to deliver against the security policy objectives outlined within the PRSP framework. The primary objective was 'to build security forces able to prevent and respond to external and internal security threats and provide an enabling environment for poverty reduction'.[7] Only activities scoring 1 or 2 had a realistic possibility of being funded under the PRSP framework.

It was important that the security sector demonstrate the progress it was already making towards both Pillar One of the PRSP and the broader PRSP process. Activities that were already being funded were included in the implementation plan; their contribution could be captured in any reporting against PRSP implementation. When the ONS submitted the NSSR implementation plan to DACO, 73 activities were determined to be of top priority out of the 148 security-related activities put forward by security sector institutions. The total cost of the activities submitted was estimated at US$93.1m. This was 55.6 per cent of the total financial requirement of Pillar One of the PRSP and 24.7 per cent of the total cost requirement for the PRSP as a whole.

Meanwhile, over at DACO, the rest of the PRSP activity matrices were facing difficulties. It was at this stage that the security and development see-saw should have swung towards 'security needs development'. Relative success had brought its own shortcomings – Sierra Leoneans were no longer worried about being raped or killed; they were concerned that their kids were not going to school, healthcare was woefully inadequate, corruption was all-pervasive and economic opportunities were in short supply.

The challenge was to build the capacity of weakened and inexperienced institutions that had the ability to bid for funding. But often these organisations lacked the capacity to know where they lacked capacity, and were part of a government that knew it needed to realign priorities, but did not know how. Rather than the security sector being the leader in enabling the environment necessary for poverty reduction to occur, it now needed to be a follower, but lead institutions such as the Anti-Corruption Commission, the National Revenue Authority, the Ministry of Mineral Resources and the Ministry of Marine Resources did not appear, for reasons of either disorganisation or disinterest, to be able to lead. This presented all concerned with a quandary – how could a set of institutions contribute to broader government when there was no broader government to which to contribute?

As mentioned earlier, it was at this stage that both the international community and the GoSL were badly caught out, for different reasons. One of the main assets of the ten-year MoU between the UK and the GoSL was that rather than being subject to the standard donor three-year bidding cycles, UK aid allocation to Sierra Leone was fixed at £40m a year for the duration of the MoU. This is a sizeable amount of money – the UK's largest aid per capita programme in the world – but once allocated it allows no flexibility for filling the development spaces created by success in other sectors. The work undertaken in the security sector, for example, created opportunities for work in trade, the diamond industry, healthcare, education and local government, but the funding was not there to take advantage of the opportunities.

The simple fact is that Sierra Leone, while over-aided by the UK, was and remains poorly served financially by other international donors, many of whom see the country as being a 'UK aid darling'. The November 2005 Consultative Group meeting,[8] designed to generate financial support for the PRSP, did not meet expectations. This left a large funding shortfall between the PRSP budget of originally over $1bn, revised to approximately $500m, and the final amount pledged (which, in turn, differed from the amount actually given). When this was coupled with a high inflation rate, very little additional money was available for developmental activity, with most of the GoSL's budget being spent on recurrent costs, mainly wages. The situation was made worse by the withdrawal of UNAMSIL at the end of 2005, and in particular the economic impact this had on the population in Freetown.

It would be wrong to apportion the blame solely to the international community. The GoSL had ample opportunity to demonstrate to sceptical donors that it had the wherewithal to implement an ambitious PRSP programme. Instead, government representatives selected to promote the PRSP opted to take a comprehensive 'PRSP road show' to international capitals, with very little thought given to policy priorities. The PRSP amounted to little more than a substantial shopping list; limited effort had been made to prioritise, or indeed link, activities, either within or between the three pillars. There was much repetition, little economies of scale achieved and no multidisciplinary approach across departments. A set of government departments were pursuing their own objectives in isolation from each other, and none had the funding necessary to do much more than pay recurrent costs. This state of affairs poses an interesting conundrum for an international donor: how does one support the policies of a government that has no policies?

The PRSP process was, in sum, a debacle. Worse still, it became clear that a potentially dangerous stalemate was brewing. With no new money appearing, the government had little interest in governing. This meant a

Chapter 6

Justice Sector Reform

Anthony Howlett-Bolton

Introduction

The purpose of this chapter is twofold: to serve as a basis for ongoing discussion on why we need to ensure that justice and security sector reform processes must complement each other; and to document progress made so far in justice and security sectors reforms in Sierra Leone from 1999 to 2007.

Given the dominant influence of the security sector, which appears sometimes to attempt to subsume the justice sector, or at least portray it as a junior partner, this chapter reflects the general approach of the Sierra Leone Justice Sector Development Programme (JSDP) by raising the profile of justice sector development while concentrating on those elements specifically allied to security.

Post-conflict support in Sierra Leone

Regardless of where a state is on the circle of democratic stability, interventions and programmes should emanate from an overarching strategic direction. Practice guidelines to establish such a strategic direction for Sierra Leone were published by the UK Department for International Development (DFID) in April 2007.[1] However, when the country was still emerging from civil war in the early 2000s, the strategic approach was less defined than it was evolutionary. Strategic direction guidelines were not evident; less sector-wide coherence existed than exists today.

With the end of hostilities in 2001, and the war declared officially over in early 2002, post-conflict support was provided by the international community. Justice and security sector support manifested itself principally as support to the Republic of Sierra Leone Armed Forces (RSLAF), the Sierra Leone Police (SLP) and, later, to the Office of National Security (ONS), the Central Intelligence and Security Unit (CISU) and the Anti-Corruption Commission (ACC). Prior to the start of the JSDP, no assistance was given to either the Ministry of Internal Affairs or the Prison Service. (Currently, these institutions still suffer from difficulties due to lack of support.)

The Relationship Between Justice and Security Sectors

Security is a cross-cutting issue. While justice and security sectors complement each other, they have both similar and different objectives and distinctly different target interests. At the same time, these two areas have come much closer together under the umbrella of SSR. Traditionally the security sector has related to national security, i.e. the stability of the state and its government, while the justice sector related to human or individual safety founded on the rights and duties of individuals according to principles determined by the rule of law. The formal security sector was/is primarily accountable to government, while the justice sector is charged, *inter alia,* with holding government accountable, which is why its independence is deemed to be essential. The justice sector works within the rules determined by civil and criminal justice systems, whereas the security sector, in extraordinary circumstances, may override ordinary standards of justice in the interest of national security.

Therefore, despite the coming together of the two agendas, the two sectors are not the same and have different emphases. It may even be dangerous to widen the definition of security to the extent that it is all-embracing – and in any case anything that becomes a definition of everything becomes a definition of nothing. While strategically there is sense that these sectors have common approaches, it is in the interest of the state for them to collaborate but be operationally separate. It must also be remembered that, generally, in countries emerging from conflict there is a mistrust of security agencies and attempts to co-locate justice and security sectors may undermine credibility further and inhibit the development of a normal democratic state.

The security and stability of a state is usually a prerequisite for development, growth, peace and justice within its borders. Often these are brought together in the arena of 'good governance'. Thus, as elsewhere, post-conflict priorities in Sierra Leone have included re-establishing basic security as a precondition for further development. UK assistance from the Africa Conflict Prevention Pool (ACPP) has contributed significantly to this objective.

In the post-war period the relationship and engagement between justice and security sectors, indeed the engagement of actors in the justice sector itself, have been difficult. This has become more significant in the move to economic growth and development, as attention has turned from PRSP Pillar One priorities of good governance, security and peace to priorities of Pillars Two and Three, relating to the promotion of pro-poor sustainable growth for food security, job creation and human development. In essence, all these areas could be described as being in competition for government and donor money. From a treasury point of view, it is a general principle that it is not acceptable for any institution to fish in two ponds at the same time.

This has been a real consideration for both the SLP and the Ministry of Internal Affairs, as inevitably they have a foot in both justice and security sectors. Both have a significant role to play in guaranteeing state security; for this reason they are key members of the state security coordinating machinery set up under the National Security and Central Intelligence Act. However, in a democracy their duty is to move away from a state security role to one of upholding the rule of law and the rights of citizens within the criminal justice system.

It should be remembered that policing goes to the heart of civic stability. It has been described as *the most fundamental relationship between citizens and the state.*[2] The police do not serve the state. A police force acceptable and accountable to the people it serves is one that is seen as an upholder of the law that protects the rights and liberties of every individual citizen, rather than as a defender of the state. History and international experience suggest that police forces which do not see themselves as part of the criminal justice system and function outside its checks and balances can themselves become security threats and instruments of oppression. ,

The relationship between the justice and security sectors is not an 'either-or' situation; rather it is a degree of balance – a trade-off of one against the other. It is clear that in a post-conflict environment the need of the state to secure itself against threats must predominate; rights of the individual are inevitably subordinated. But as society evolves into the economic growth and development period, the rights of the individual are reasserted and predominate.

It could be suggested that this is principally an academic issue that manifests itself in strategic directions from an international donor perspective. However, in practice funding follows strategy. This evolution of emphasis between national security needs and individual security rights, and thus the relationship between justice and security sectors, has real impact in

> …the arguments over which organisation belongs to what sector have put pressures on domestic partners to 'place' themselves within the context of UK-defined policies, rather than within national policy and budgeting processes, in order to access different UK resources. This seems to contradict the benefit of developing sector-wide approaches, which should not add burdens for partner governments. Under SSAJ [security sector and accessible justice] policy, criminal justice institutions are considered together in order to enhance the effectiveness of the criminal justice system. As the gatekeeper of the criminal justice system, policing is linked to justice sector policies and priorities. Prisons depend on effective criminal justice system to manage their population.

As part of the development of the justice sector reform strategy, national partners have come to an agreement on the recognition of the justice sector.[8] The former vice president, who chaired the Justice Sector Strategic Planning Committee, requested the preparation of a justice sector budget aligned to the medium-term expenditure framework. The Ministry of Finance has recognised the justice sector as separate and stressed the need to prepare a separate sector budget.

Holistic Development of the JSDP

The contextual background[9] against which the JSDP was created was that of a state emerging from a civil war that lasted from 1991 until 2002 and ranking 177 out of 177 countries in the 2006 Human Development Index. The Truth and Reconciliation Commission confirmed the impact of justice system weaknesses on the civil war and the need for the post-war transition to progress towards re-establishing the rule of law and making justice accessible.

The JSDP was built on a history of UK support to the police and judiciary in Sierra Leone, with a view to moving to a coordinated sector-wide approach. It was designed in line with the UK's strategy for Sierra Leone:[10] to establish a peaceful and stable country through, among other things, 'improved security', 'improved governance' and 'fostering a just and inclusive economy and society'. It was also in line with DFID's safety, security and accessible justice policy, which aims to 'make justice systems work better, especially for poor people in ways that are appropriate to the local culture and within available resources'.[11]

The JSDP was designed in June 2002, approved in April 2004 and began implementation in March 2005. This timeframe created significant start-up challenges, with some stakeholders impatient to see activities starting and others concerned that support for the CCSSP, in particular, would cease. The JSDP incorporated elements of both the CCSSP and the Law Development Programme and inherited continued funding of commonwealth judges and prosecutors and a legal draftsman post.

The DFID-sponsored Law Development Programme was a relatively small stand-alone project of £3–4 million launched in October 2003, with a view to addressing three main issues facing the legal profession in Sierra Leone.

- The ability, capacity and working effectiveness of the judiciary, including higher courts and the local courts applying customary law
- Reform of the legal code to reflect contemporary needs better, and the presentation of this redrafted legislation to Parliament through the Ministry of Justice
- Training of all levels of legal personnel, including High Court judges

Institutional strengthening was achieved through refurbishing the main Law Courts building in Freetown, restoring the three provincial High Courts and building and refurbishing magistrates' courts in both the capital and the provinces. It worked on reducing case backlogs, building up the court registry system, restoring stenographic record systems and updating the Law Courts library. It provided the law officers' department with essential logistical support, updated the library and storage equipment and improved records management at the administrator and registrar general's office. Local courts were provided with limited logistical support, such as uniforms, insignia for local course officials, stationery, secure storage cupboards and bicycles.

It is quite clear that the GoSL remains committed to justice and security sector reform, which it sees as integral to conflict prevention and poverty reduction. This commitment is reflected in the national policy framework for the justice sector approved by a steering committee, and government reform policies stated in the PRSP. The PRSP sets out the government's plans to tackle poverty in the medium term, cites rule of law and respect for human rights as key components of governance and includes as a priority objective 'improved administration of justice and human rights'. Pillar One (promoting good governance, security and peace) includes actions to improve access to justice for the poor, strengthening the SLP, ensuring respect for human rights, empowerment of women and strengthening the participation of civil society. Pillar Three (human development) includes action to improve support to children and tackle gender-based violence.

The five-year contract awarded by DFID to the British Council to implement the JSDP contained a built-in review after the initial two-year phase. Contract implementation began in March 2005. Unlike the CCSSP, the International Military Assistance Training Team (IMATT) and the Sierra Leone Security Sector Programme (SILSEP), the JSDP was designed to be led by the government. This had implications for the JSDP's ability to redirect its spending without express approval of the JSDP steering committee, which was not always appreciated outside the programme. Given the mandate, during the inception phase partnership arrangements between the government leadership, civil society and JSDP staff were established. Management structures were set up, including a secretariat. Led by a programme director and a programme manager, the JSDP management team were divided into three outward-facing components – safety and security, administration of justice and informal justice (including all non-state actors) – supported by a monitoring, evaluation and research component as well as the engagement of an infrastructure development expert.

The steering committee and a task force were crucial in the development and implementation of the JSDP. Without their active support, the entire programme stood little chance of succeeding. They were actively engaged in the formulation and approval of the work plan and its implementation.

The first meeting under the JSDP was held in May 2005 to begin prioritising work and agree activities and tasks. As indicated earlier, following some impatience expressed by partners over extended consultation and design stages, an emphasis was placed on immediate implementation of a wide range of interventions across the sector, including infrastructure projects. The willingness to engage quickly in agreed initiatives was crucial for building relationships, trust and credibility.

During task force meetings, the role of civil society in the JSDP was discussed at some length. While there was civil society representation in the process, it was thought to be limited. Given that there are many different civil society groups with an interest in justice issues, it was decided to set up a separate committee of civil society representatives – the Civil Society Justice Sector Coordinating Group. This group met for the first time in June 2005, and sent representatives to the task force to speak on behalf of civil society as a whole.

The heads of the institutions, represented in the steering committee, each nominated two representatives for regular attendance at task force meetings, with a mandate to participate in the direction of the programme as it developed, review progress and identify any pressing issues that needed to be addressed. They were also instrumental in ensuring that the implementation phase of the programme was developed in line with a sectoral approach to justice budgeting and planning. The justice sector reform and implementation plan brought with it a sector-wide functioning coordination unit and realignment of the steering committee and task force into a justice sector leadership and a technical working group.[12]

The JSDP team, with inputs from the task force, developed an inception report, which included an operational strategy, a log frame, objectives, performance indicators, key reform areas for the initial two-year phase and a detailed work plan for the first six months. The inception report was approved by the steering committee and DFID in July 2005.

In summary, the first year provided largely 'stand-alone' assistance, with government involvement resting primarily in planning and oversight functions, through the task force and steering committees. Of particular note were strengthened government involvement, growing acceptance of a justice sector[13] and improved relationships and credibility.

Building on these achievements, an increased focus was given to the primary objective: the development of a costed justice sector reform strategy (JSRS) aligned with the government's PRSP medium-term expenditure framework and annual budgeting processes, and with the donor objective of moving away from 'stand-alone' assistance. The JSRS was adopted in December 2007 and is designed to lead to a sector-wide approach that is fully integrated within government processes. By the end of the JSDP in 2010, it is envisaged that consideration should be given to supporting the JSRS through sector budget support.

Capacity in the justice sector reflects weaknesses apparent in the wider government. A recommended objective for the GoSL reform strategy is to support both state and non-state justice systems operating in Sierra Leone, and ensure that both work fairly and effectively to provide a real choice for the majority of people. Each system will have its own advantages and disadvantages and both need support, even if the state system will inevitably require a greater share of financial resources.

To achieve sustainable and affordable change, work needs to be undertaken across the board to develop and enable the capacity of the constituent parts of the sector. This takes time. While accepting that it is a long-term process, it can be augmented by 'quick wins', but it would be unwise to place too much store on these. In essence, significant discernible impact on the ground is unlikely to be found at the early stages of a developmental sector-wide project, but some early progress is usually possible.

The Migration from the CCSSP to the JSDP

Commonwealth Community Safety and Security Project

As an extension to the original Commonwealth Police Development Task Force, from 1999 the UK government assisted in the rebuilding and development of the SLP via a programme known as the Commonwealth Community Safety and Security Project (CCSSP). The CCSSP programme ended in June 2005, some four months after the commencement of the JSDP. In the absence of functioning institutions, at inception the CCSSP faced significant challenges in a country suffering from violent conflict, threats to life, internal displacement and limited rule of law.

In 1997–1998, prior to the CCSSP, the police was a force in crisis and out of control. This was evidenced by a lack of professionalism, discrimination, patronage and lack of effective leadership. There was no routine strategic thinking and a total lack of vision. Daily work was undertaken on an 'as usual' basis emanating from a rank-conscious military-style force with no reference to either modern-day policing or planning. There was neither transparency nor accountability. Everything was secretive.

While in an ideal world consideration should be given to the long-term consequences of intervention, there is something of a dichotomy for those charged with implementation. In order to stabilise a country and have visibility in the short term, there is a need to react quickly and provide logistical support on the ground – such as communications equipment and vehicles. This requires considerable short-term donor investment on capital provision. The difficulty is that once donor support is rightly refocused into other areas, the financial burden remaining for the Ministry of Finance in terms of both recurrent and capital replacement expenditure is not affordable and the provision becomes unsustainable. This is something of a double blow, as by then the relevant institution (in this case the SLP) has become totally dependent upon contributions by external actors. Withdrawal of international funding inevitably leads to short-term paralysis and degradation of service, with a real danger of relapse to the *status quo ante*. Given the need to shift from a post-conflict scenario to one of economic growth and development, there was a need to refocus support to the SLP and be more inclusive of the wider justice sector.

In the first three months of the programme, during the inception phase, the JSDP recognised that significant progress had been made by the SLP over the previous six years, and also that the sector-wide mandate of the JSDP was different to the institutional mandate of the CCSSP. This inevitably influenced what could continue to be funded, and therefore required a different approach to the SLP. A migration plan was submitted to the inspector general of police, the minister of internal affairs and DFID, acknowledging the fact that initial assessment on the ground did not seem to be in accord with the posited position advanced in London on the post-conflict/economic growth and development continuum. After consultation with the inspector general on the impact of the CCSSP interventions and consultants used by the programme, CCSSP elements closely allied to task force priorities were recommended to continue under the JSDP. These included strategic planning and management, operational intelligence activities, crime management and training, support to finance and administration systems, and support to training and development, especially for middle- and lower-ranking officers.[14] This left something of a gap in security-style operations that needed to be addressed separately under DFID's SILSEP. This added to the tensions previously alluded to, and had to be carefully managed.

During the civil war the people of Sierra Leone lost faith in the justice sector and the police. The last DFID output to purpose review on the CCSSP made explicit reference to the fact that without greater management visibility and continued emphasis and restatement of SLP purpose, policing style and values, some officers could revert to their old ways[15]. Additionally, the safety and security review made particular reference to the need for strengthening devolved power, authority and, most importantly, responsibility to local unit commanders.

Policing, in its widest sense, is one of the means by which law and order and the rule of law are respected and maintained. Within the paradigm of normal rights-based policing (rather than threats-based policing), a community policing style takes precedence. Local needs policing (LNP) is the designation for community policing in Sierra Leone. It is designed to meet the expectations and needs of local communities, and reflects national and international standards and objectives. It is delivered locally through an empowered local command unit.

Therefore, given the need to ensure a policing style that emphasised partnership and quality service delivery over confrontation, the migration proposals from the CCSSP to the JSDP in particular emphasised that the LNP was central to the shift the SLP needed to make from post-conflict safety and security stabilisation to being a mature modern-state organisation dealing effectively with law and order.

LNP was reinforced as the chosen vehicle to deliver these principles and is strongly featured throughout the SLP strategic plan. All JSDP-funded SLP interventions flowed from implementation of this concept as a mechanism for providing access to justice, effective oversight and accountability for the SLP. (It should be stressed, however, that for the SLP to be effective in terms of community policing, the current inability of the Ministry of Internal Affairs to exercise proper oversight must continue to be addressed.)

Elections are fundamental to the democratic process, but inevitably can divert attention from developmental progress and halt it for some time. One can either take the view that post-election developmental activity should be suspended or try to maintain development progress, albeit at a reduced level. While this is a judgement call, DFID and the JSDP took the position that it would be unwise to throttle back on the development momentum; better to be ambitious and suffer a temporary shortfall than to reduce development activity. Nevertheless, in order to militate against any potential negative impact or lack of focus during the pre-election and election periods, the JSDP continued to work closely with staff and officials to ensure continuity.

A key element of the SLP's transformation is its change management programmes, which seek to initiate, implement and monitor organisational and operational interventions designed to improve SLP's effectiveness. When the JSDP took over responsibility for the provision of technical assistance at the end of the CCSSP, the draft three-year strategic plan for the SLP was well advanced. At the request of the JSDP, focus on LNP was enhanced. This LNP focus secured final approval from the Police Council in 2006 and was published, together with an abridged version for wider circulation. The general approach reflected the need for balanced policing within a democratic context, while identifying the SLP as a main strategic partner within the justice sector and also recognising the SLP's security role. Under the guidance of the JSDP, technical assistance was provided to assist the SLP to develop the necessary tactical and operational plans to underpin the strategic plan. The JSDP also provided assistance in the development of a communications strategy that would enable the plan to be understood and delivered to the grassroots level.

The SLP is currently engaged in a number of change management projects. While each has its merits, there is a need for rationalisation and focus if the outcomes are to be realised. Challenges still remain in implementation of projects within the SLP. Project team meetings are still infrequent, with project managers preferring to develop and implement the projects on their own. There are frequent personnel transfers that result in team discontinuity and make project implementation difficult.

Considerable training and development occurred during the life of the CCSSP, resulting in pockets of excellence, particularly with respect to the SLP executive management board and other senior officers. Universal concern that this quality could not be found at lower levels in the organisation was supported by the conclusion of a DFID output to purpose review, which noted an insufficient emphasis on the lack of management and supervisory skills at middle and junior levels of the organisation[16].

A lesson learned for the future is to expose middle and junior managers in the service to training opportunities so as to ensure that progress and direction of the force are not dissipated at the operational level. As with the wider sector, it is also important to ensure that elements of the service do not receive a disproportionate amount of technical assistance and support, thus causing a training imbalance.

As a result of CCSSP activities, the SLP is well placed to move reform forward. It is unfortunate that the same cannot be said for most of the remainder of the justice sector, which has not attracted funding support during the main phase of the post-conflict environment.

Conclusion

In conclusion, the way forward must be coherent. The framework for future development must flow from the justice sector reform strategy and the structures that support it. To be affordable and sustainable, future development must be led and administered by relevant Sierra Leone institutions acting in concert and supported with technical assistance from the JSDP. The heads of the justice institutions are quite right to insist that donor aid be coordinated and not forced upon them inappropriately. This is all to the good, but this coherent framework approach emanating from the JSRS will require the newly formed justice sector coordination unit to fulfil its functions appropriately.

Notes

1 Explanatory Note on Security and Access to Justice for the Poor, DFID practice paper, April 2007.

2 Mitchell B. Reiss, Director, Policy Planning Staff, Testimony to the US Helsinki.Commission, Washington, DC, 16 March 2004.

3 Explanatory Note on Security and Access to Justice for the Poor, DFID practice paper, April 2007.

4 Unpublished briefing note, Office of National Security, Freetown, Sierra Leone, 2007.

5 OECD DAC (2004) *Security Systems Reform*, OECD DAC.

6 Explanatory Note on Security and Access to Justice for the Poor, DFID practice paper, April 2007.

7 Output to Purpose Review of JSDP, March 2007.

8 In Sierra Leone the justice sector is seen to comprise the Ministry of Justice, Ministry of Internal Affairs, Ministry of Social Welfare, Ministry of Local Government, judiciary, police, prisons, Law Reform Commission, Judicial and Legal Service Commission and the Office of the Ombudsman.

9 JSDP Output to Purpose Review, February 2007.

10 Sierra Leone – Medium Term HMG Strategy, February 2003.

11 SSAJ for All – Putting Policy into Practice, DFID, September 2002.

12 See Justice Sector Reform Strategy and Implementation Plan, Chapter 4.

13 The justice sector was formally recognised by the government as a separate entity and incorporated into the national budgetary processes by the Ministry of Finance in October 2006 as an identifiable budget line.

14 Project Completion Report, September 2007, Sierra Leone Police Vehicles and Communications Project, and the Sierra Leone Police Infrastructure Project.

15 Output to Purpose Review, 30 May – 6 June, Sierra Leone Community Safety Security Project, DFID, 2003.

16 Joint DFID and FCO Synthesis and Review of UK Funded Safety and Security Programmes, Sierra Leone Case Study, DFID, November 2004. This was also reinforced by the Project Completion Report, September 2007, Sierra Leone Police Vehicles and Communications Project, and the Sierra Leone Police Infrastructure Project.

Part III

Sierra Leone Perspectives

Chapter 7

Governance and Security Sector Reform

Emmanuel B. Osho Coker

Introduction

Upon achieving independence in 1961, Sierra Leone inherited from the British colonial administration public administration institutions that delivered generally effective services, including maintenance of law and order. However, by the early 1970s service performance had declined; public institutions were weak and poor governance prevailed. In particular, the decision in 1972 to dissolve the district councils, which had provided popular representation through direct elections, heralded the over-centralisation of power and resources in the capital city of Freetown. This situation undermined the institution of local government and deprived the rural population of participation in the political decision-making process at district and chiefdom levels. The judiciary also went through an integrity crisis, and was characterised by poor administration of justice.

The rebel war, which started in 1991, aggravated the situation and resulted in destruction of the country's social, economic and physical infrastructure. Sierra Leone went through many difficulties and challenges in the succeeding years. A military government held power from April 1992 until March 1996, when it was replaced by the democratically elected government of President Ahmad Tejan Kabbah. In February 1997 a national strategy for good governance and public service reform was prepared by three national consultants with funding from the UK Overseas Development Administration (ODA) and the UN Development Programme (UNDP). Among other things, the strategy recognised that if democratic governance was to be effective, there was an urgent need for reform of the entire criminal justice sector, including police, judiciary and prison systems. It also identified the need to reduce the size of the armed forces to a lean, manageable, loyal, efficient and disciplined unit; provide adequate training for the armed forces to protect life, property and the integrity of the state; and improve military/civilian relations.

In May 1997 there was yet another military coup which ousted Kabbah's government. The country experienced a reign of terror by the Armed Forces Revolutionary Council (AFRC) until February 1998, when a subregional intervention force of the Economic Community of West African States Monitoring Group (ECOMOG) forcibly removed it from power. The civil war raged on, causing untold hardship and misery for the people of Sierra Leone.

Following the restoration of relative stability in the country, with assistance from a UN peacekeeping force (UNAMSIL), the government declared in February 2002 that peace had been achieved. At the time of UNAMSIL's departure in December 2005, the government's authority had been re-established and public sector institutions were functioning again, albeit with severe capacity and structural constraints. The Governance and Civil Service Reform Programme (GCSRP) now in place has the objective of rebuilding the government of Sierra Leone's capacity to provide services and enhance the welfare of its citizens by implementing a number of key public service reform programmes through the Governance Reform Secretariat.

The Public Sector Institutional Environment

Public sector governance in Sierra Leone is saddled with various problems, including cumbersome and outdated procedures; obsolete regulations which are mostly ignored; a paucity of skilled managerial, professional and technical personnel; woefully inadequate civil service incentive systems resulting in poor performance, brain drain and absence of a serious work ethic; weak accountability and transparency; haphazard, unsystematic and uncoordinated human resource development; an unnecessarily bloated civil service, especially at lower levels; unavailability and/or inaccessibility of physical resources; financial constraints; lack of accurate and accessible personnel information; and low morale, lax discipline and sporadic attendance.

In October 1998 the UK Department for International Development (DFID) funded a diagnostic study of the civil service in Sierra Leone. The erstwhile Ministry of Internal Affairs and Local Administration was one of the ministries selected for the study. At that time, the ministry had oversight over police, prison, fire and immigration services. However, there was lack of capacity within the ministry to provide analytical advice to the minister on policy and technical issues. A Commonwealth police development task force had proposed that a police department be set up in the ministry to provide effective police services advice to the minister. The consultants undertaking the diagnostic study discussed the proposal with the permanent secretary, who not only supported the idea but further proposed the establishment of a police policy secretariat in the ministry. Out of a total of 14 ministry reviews to date, the security-sector-related ministries covered are defence (2003) and internal affairs (2007).

As individual management and functional reviews progressed in key ministries, weaknesses were identified in the overall government policy-making and implementation machinery that contributed to a lack of a comprehensive and coherent strategic direction across the architecture of ministry structures. The joint government/donor task force on capacity-building reviewed the entire structure of government ministries, departments and agencies (MDAs) and recommended where rationalisation, amalgamation, transfer of responsibilities or other management models, including the poverty reduction strategy paper (PRSP), would support more effective reform implementation.

In early 2006 a horizontal review was conducted to identify an appropriate government-wide structure that would facilitate the functions and mandates that enable public administration to perform effectively the necessary core functions of government. The study revealed a high level of overlap in both functions and statutory frameworks across ministries and commissions. It also identified statutory overlaps between the Ministry of Defence and the Ministry of Internal Affairs in the area of national security intelligence. The report, which recommended blueprint structures for both the general architecture of government and individual ministries, is still awaiting submission to the Steering Committee on Good Governance.

Civil Service and Governance Reform Impact on the Security Sector

It has been acknowledged in various reports, including the governance and corruption survey of 2002, the Sierra Leone Vision 2025 and the PRSP, that there can be no meaningful and sustainable development in Sierra Leone without adequate security. Equally, it is accepted that peace can only be sustained if public institutions are reformed to make them responsive to the needs of the people, particularly by reducing poverty and improving the level of human development. In the threat analysis contained in the 2005 Sierra Leone security sector review report, some of the threats identified relate to the efficiency and effectiveness of service delivery. They include bad governance, corruption, lack of effective implementation and monitoring of government policies, an over-centralised political and administrative system, ill-equipped and poorly paid security forces and institutions and poor service conditions.

Considerable work has been undertaken through the GCSRP to create a lean, efficient and performance-oriented civil service that provides effective service delivery. A joint government/DFID annual review of the GCSRP, conducted in May 2006, assessed the programme as having registered significant progress in terms of technical preparation for the reconstruction and reform of the public service in Sierra Leone. The following initiatives are geared towards addressing capacity issues that will make the state administration function effectively:

- A diagnostic study of the architecture of government of Sierra Leone (a horizontal review across ministries)
- Management and functional reviews of 14 ministries
- Ongoing work to create a human resource management office (HRMO)
- Strengthening of the Cabinet secretariat
- Introduction of new regulations and rules and a civil service code
- A records management improvement programme has already completed the reconciliation of personnel records to staff pin codes (used for the payroll) in the Establishment Secretary's Office and the Ministries of Health, Education and Agriculture; it is now reviewing and strengthening personnel files and linking them to payroll verification
- Development of a training policy and implementation plan, approved by the Cabinet in April 2007
- Resuscitation of the Civil Service Training College and the Institute of Public Administration and Management
- Design of a comprehensive pay and grading strategy and a public sector pay policy framework approved by the cabinet in January 2007
- Development of a draft public sector reform strategy, now awaiting consideration by the Steering Committee on Good Governance for onward transmission to the Cabinet
- A selected market salary survey, conducted in February 2006.

The expected outcomes of these reform initiatives are:

- Strengthened national, regional and provincial institutional framework
- Improved coordination, resource mobilisation, delivery and monitoring of the poverty reduction strategy programme and strategic development of Sierra Leone
- Senior managerial capacity for policy formulation, systems design, implementation and support for decentralised service delivery
- An improved institutional environment capable of retaining capacity and nurturing communication, cross-fertilisation and policy development initiatives.

It is pertinent to mention that while some achievements have been realised, progress has been slow in implementing the overall vision for civil service reform. While the need for attitudinal change is still evident, the problem of the government's inability to pay living wages continues to act as a demotivating factor and a disincentive to attracting the right types of skills into the civil service. The problem is compounded by the existence of project implementation units staffed by contract personnel whose remuneration is more attractive than that of other civil servants. This disparity in remuneration packages creates resentment among civil servants who are expected to work with and understudy the contract personnel; very little transfer of skills is taking place between the two groups.

In 2003 the government decided to tackle this problem by restructuring public service management levels to create a senior executive service (SES). The SES would consist of highly competent senior civil servants selected on a transparent basis through a competitive assessment process. They would initiate, sustain and manage proactive public sector changes, promote reform efforts and enhance the strategic output of government. The SES would consist of civil service grades 11–14, who would receive enhanced salary and other types of reward linked to performance. The complete pay package incorporating allowances and monetising all forms of services and 'in-kind' payments would be extended to the rest of the public service. Key issues pertaining to the SES are now being discussed, including the abolition of dual hierarchies, integration of senior management posts in ministries into a single management structure and the integration of project implementation unit or contract officer posts in ministries into the civil service.

Specific Reforms in Security-Sector-Related Ministries

Ministry of Defence

Through a bilateral agreement between the governments of Sierra Leone and the UK to train the Republic of Sierra Leone Armed Forces and reorganise the Ministry of Defence (MoD), the MoD was established in January 2002 as a joint civilian/military institution. According to its mission statement, its goal is 'To formulate, implement, monitor and evaluate strategic defence policy for the new Republic of Sierra Leone Armed Forces that is effective and fostered within the framework of democratic government.' In October/November 2003 a joint team of Sierra Leonean and UK consultants carried out a management and functional review of the organisation, structures and processes of the MoD. The recommendations contained in the report were approved by the Cabinet in September 2004; implementation is ongoing. Key recommendations that impact on the security sector include the following.

- The Constitution of Sierra Leone 1991 should be amended to provide for a single joint force command; the Royal Sierra Leone Military Forces Act of 1961 (the country's primary defence sector legislation) should be reviewed, consolidated and updated to meet present-day requirements.
- MoD development of a personnel policy that covers civilian staff.
- Development of an annual management plan setting out key MoD objectives, priorities and resource inputs, as well as timescales and assigned responsibilities for delivery of specific activities.
- Budgetary structures should be reviewed to indicate proposed expenditures within each directorate. In addition, processes should be put in place to scrutinise, review and propose needs and priorities, as well as procedures to monitor and manage activity or programme performance against budget.
- The internal audit process should be strengthened.
- The procurement process should be reviewed in order to simplify and reduce current time-consuming procedures and create a more manageable system.
- The present MoD committee structure should be reviewed and guidelines established for future committee operations.
- An appraisal reporting system should be introduced at the earliest opportunity.

- The Establishment Secretary's Office should undertake an evaluation of senior civilian posts to assess and determine the appropriate grading for the positions in question.

Although the report acknowledged that the mix of military and civilian staff operating together with common goals epitomises the new working relationship in Sierra Leone's defence sector, it also pointed out two areas of concern. The first is the heavy reliance on the expertise and support provided by the International Military Assistance Training Team (IMATT) set up by the UK in 2001; the second concerns the wide disparities existing between civilian and military staff in terms of grading and remuneration.

In the area of communications, the report recommended that links between military and civil society organisations should be reactivated in order to improve mutual understanding and increase public trust.

Concerning accommodation and material resources, the MoD is comparatively better accommodated and better resourced than other MDAs; morale seems to be slightly higher among its staff. There is a general feeling that MoD reforms have been more successful than those of other MDAs.

Ministry of Internal Affairs

A management and functional review of the Ministry of Internal Affairs (MIA) was carried out in September/October 2006. This ministry is classified as one of the key ministries in Sierra Leone, primarily because of its strategic oversight of agencies involved in the maintenance of internal safety and security. (The ministry is responsible for the Sierra Leone Police, Prisons Department, Immigration Department, National Fire Fighting Force and National Registration Secretariat.) As stated in the review report, 'Successive changes in structure and allocation of responsibilities to outside agencies have given rise to a strengthening of these institutions' autonomy, whilst inadvertently undermining the relevance of the central role of the MIA.' It further states 'It could be said that the significant development of agencies such as the Police negates the need for the MIA to continue in its present form. However, there is need for a permanent civil regulatory framework and a means of providing adequate political oversight.' A number of measures were recommended to revitalise the MIA to enable it to fulfil the role of strategic coordination of the sector. Some of the key recommendations include:

- Strengthening the senior management team as a priority
- Revising and updating the statutory framework governing MIA operations and making them relevant to the present day
- Revising of functions and organisational structures
- Clarifying the MIA's relationship with its partner security and safety institutions
- Using the new Policy Development and Strategic Planning Directorate to lead the MIA in its planning and budget prioritisation processes
- Revamping relationship management processes with stakeholders and the public
- Ceding the decentralised functions of the ministry to other appropriate agencies or institutions
- Review of existing staff inventory and staffing arrangements
- Strengthening human resource management functions and revamping records and information management
- Identifying priority equipment needs
- Creating institutional arrangements for managing change and change processes

While these recommendations were awaiting consideration by the Steering Committee on Good Governance and Cabinet, the 2007 presidential and parliamentary elections established a new government under the leadership of Ernest Bai Koroma. Subsequently, the configuration of MDAs has witnessed a transformation involving, *inter alia*, the merging of the MIA with the erstwhile local government ministry to form a new Ministry of Internal Affairs and Rural Development. The new ministry is still responsible for the aforementioned security agencies; as a supervising ministry it still has the statutory authority to fulfil its mandate effectively. However, as stated in the review report, the present role of the Office of National Security *vis-à-vis* the ministry regarding security coordination is not clear and the ministry appears to be marginalised. It has been recommended that the ministry and the various institutions under its aegis should work collaboratively in defining their respective roles and responsibilities to facilitate effective coordination of security directives and policies. The boundaries of the ministry's oversight responsibility should also be clearly defined.

Concerning the MIA's relationship with other MDAs, it has been recommended that a core directorate should be developed to act as a liaison with security agencies. The ministry should not only be able to coordinate and integrate national responses to riots, disasters, drug trafficking and other security threats; it should also be able to influence and determine the appropriateness of security and safety policy and activity. In 2008 the Governance Reform Secretariat conducted an institutional appraisal of the newly combined Ministry of Internal Affairs, Local Government and Rural Development to ensure efficient and effective transition and development of organisational structures which support the combined mandate. Within the security sector's national strategic policy framework, the new combined ministry will take the lead in thwarting one of the threats to good governance – the existence of an over-centralised political/administrative system – in order to pursue the national vision of a decentralised public and local government administrative system. The ministry will also partner with other MDAs to establish the national vision for strong political will, effective border security, a safe and secure environment, an efficient justice system and well-trained, well-equipped and highly motivated security forces.

One issue also worth noting is that, with the enactment of the Local Government Act of 2004, district offices have been closed and their functions transferred to local councils and the provincial secretary's office at regional headquarters. One of the functions transferred to the provincial secretary's office is supervision and monitoring of chiefdom councils, including appointing and training chiefdom police, resolving disputes and maintaining law and order. During the management and functional review of the erstwhile Ministry of Local Government and Community Development, conducted in September/October 2004, discussions with local stakeholders revealed concerns that chiefs do not encourage their police to take a professional approach; in many cases they do not pay them a regular salary. This is not conducive to the promotion of local democracy and the rule of law, and could lead to friction with local councils/ councillors. The review report recommended that the ministry should conduct a study of the chiefdom police, persuade the government to develop and articulate a clear policy on their role and remove any current uncertainties about their operations. The amalgamation of the two ministries dealing with security and decentralisation provides a unique opportunity for this issue to be examined in depth.

Conclusion

It is mentioned elsewhere in this chapter that some of the security threats identified are connected with the efficiency and effectiveness of service

purpose of defending imperial interests. What is known today as the RSLAF evolved from the Royal West Africa Frontier Force. At the country's independence in 1961, the force was known as the Royal Sierra Leone Military Forces (RSLMF) and was under the command of a UK officer, Brigadier R. D. Blackie. Independence did not immediately affect the structure of Sierra Leone's armed forces, which resembled in all important respects the UK military structure.

Before the conflict erupted in 1991, Sierra Leone's armed forces could be described as a ceremonial and conservative army of 3,500 personnel. While there was an outward show of pretence, professionalism and efficiency were lacking. Nonetheless, despite its internal diversity, the army remained united. Recruiting and training were carried out on an *ad hoc* basis; training by foreign sources (the UK, Egypt, the US, China, Ghana, Nigeria and Tanzania) was the norm.

In spite of its unity and its training by foreigners, the armed forces exhibited a widespread lack of discipline. Recruiting mechanisms were often political: the so-called 'card system' allowed politicians and the powerful to award cards that guaranteed entry into the military. Merit mattered, but not nearly as much as personal loyalty and conformity. Although a core of professional and committed officers tried to maintain standards, they were in a distinct minority. The army lacked strength, capability, motivation and equipment. (At the time, the only weapons the army could boast were 12.7 Chinese machine guns, general-purpose machine guns, light machine guns, 81mm mortars, rocket-propelled grenades and tubes as support weapons.)

The pre-war army was an army of foot soldiers; it was neither motorised nor mechanised and had no armour or air support. It had no specialised troops or special operations equipment, and suffered from exceptionally stifling political control. Its ability to respond to internal and external threats was practically non-existent. In addition, the army during the 1960s was polarised between the southern- and eastern-based Sierra Leone People's Party (SLPP) and the northern- and western-based All People's Congress (APC). This dichotomy did not contribute to effective coordination of forces.

In the months before the 1967 general elections, several senior northern and western area officers were arrested for allegedly plotting to overthrow the SLPP government headed by Sir Albert Margai. They included Major M. S. Tarawallie, who later became a major general and force commander, Brigadier John Bangura, Majors Farrah Jawara, Seray Wurie and George Caulker, who later became a colonel. In 1967 the SLPP became the first party to introduce the army into politics in Sierra Leone after losing power in elections that year. The SLPP would not accept defeat, and inspired the incumbent force commander, Brigadier David Lansana, to stage a military coup, without success. When the country achieved republican status on 19 April 1971, the Royal Sierra Leone Military Forces were renamed the Republic of Sierra Leone Military Force by an act of fiat. It was a single service until the addition of a naval wing in 1979.

The APC government under President Siaka Stevens appointed the force commander and inspector general of police as members of Parliament. As war erupted in 1991, the military command structure was overthrown and military coups were staged, first by junior officers and later by soldiers.

The armed forces – 1991–1997

The Sierra Leone armed conflict, which started in 1991 and ended in 2002, was the product of many years of state failure and depredation. It was rooted in bad governance, consistent violation of basic human rights and endemic poverty. Government accountability was non-existent, political expression and dissent had been crushed, each regime had become increasingly impervious to the wishes and needs of the people. Democracy and the rule of law had ceased to exist. By 1991 Sierra Leone was a deeply divided society simmering on the edge of anarchy.

As a consequence, the army and the people were not prepared for the rebel war. The army was ill-equipped and badly led. Many of the card bearers deserted; many others stayed in the Freetown area. The government of the day, and subsequent governments, both military and civilian, had no alternative but to recruit hurriedly to fill the gap in personnel; consequently, selection and training of the 1991 intake of officers were poor.

In 1995, under the National Provisional Ruling Council (NPRC), the defence headquarters was established with a newly created air wing. This limited restructuring initiative, carried out by a military regime that had achieved power through a coup, resulted in the elevation of the head of the military to chief of defence staff. The RSLMF was officially renamed the Armed Forces of the Republic of Sierra Leone.

Since there were no criteria for the recruitment of other ranks or for screening to exclude recruits with criminal records, the resulting attacks on civilians were predictable. Allegations began to surface that gross human rights violations were taking place: men were robbed, beaten or killed and women were abused and raped by soldiers who came to be known as *sobels* (meaning soldiers by day and rebels by night). This led to the loss of trust of the civilian population that the army was supposed to protect. The situation between soldiers and civilians was aggravated further with the emergence of the Kamajors.[1] It is no secret that in this anarchy, civilians captured soldiers and burned them alive.

By the end of this brutal war, nearly 50,000 Sierra Leoneans had lost their lives, thousands had been maimed and a quarter of the population had been made refugees. A similar number had been internally displaced, the economy was in shambles and poverty was deeply entrenched. Hatred, vengeance and a culture of violence further divided communities; the country ranked in the lowest position in the UN Human Development Index.

From 1996 – Democratic elections and military coup

The democratic government elected in 1996 and subsequent military rule of the NPRC were unable to stabilise the country sufficiently. In addition, the new SLPP government had great problems understanding and handling the post-NPRC army in 1996–1997; there was savage fighting between the Kamajors and the army in 1995–1996. Initial armed forces restructuring was therefore badly handled and led directly to a coup by the Armed Forces Revolutionary Council (AFRC) in 1997.

Because of the politicisation of the military, undisciplined, poorly trained and ill-equipped soldiers put the country at risk. No effective opposition was organised and the AFRC coup succeeded. The country plunged into chaos and anarchy until March 1998, when the Economic Community of West African States (ECOWAS) restored the democratically elected government to power through its Nigerian-led Monitoring Group (ECOMOG). At the end of the war, the armed forces ushered in a new set of soldiers who had been promised they would be in charge of the army within the following five years. The SLPP government proved to be too weak to resist such politicisation of the military.

The fragile peace in Sierra Leone collapsed in January 1999, when remnants of the AFRC and the RUF attacked Freetown because they felt that the SLPP government had not honoured the Conakry Peace Accord relating to amnesty. After coming back from exile in early 1998, the SLPP government oversaw the execution of 24 senior officers who had been involved in the AFRC coup. Plans were also under way to execute 72 civilians found guilty of treason, including the minister of information and broadcasting in the APC government. There is a firm belief among senior officers that this plan to get rid of undesirables would have been far more extensive and protracted without the presence of IMATT. There was vehement national and international condemnation of these gross violations of human rights.

After the SLPP government was restored in 1998, it resumed the armed forces restructuring process. The Nigerian-led remnants of the indigenous officer corps began to recruit the 'New Army' from social groups that were known to have been anti-military. Partly in reaction to the 'illiterate' officers staging the 1997 coup, much emphasis was placed on educational standards. The 1999 recruitment process took place in two ways, the first dominated by the Nigerians and the second by Vice-President Joe Demby and Minister of Defence Samuel Hinga Norman. The entry of these officers coincided with the death of the Nigerian chief of defence staff, General Maxwell Khobe. A change in Nigerian government resulted in a sharp loss of Nigerian interest in Sierra Leone and support to the SLPP government; withdrawal of ECOMOG from the country began. The Nigerians were accused of double standards, engaging in diamond smuggling and collaborating with the RUF, thereby prolonging the war and preventing UN troops from working effectively. ECOMOG was therefore initially integrated into UNAMSIL.

At this time, President Tejan Kabbah was considering the idea of disbanding the entire army and following the model of Haiti, which has a police force with expanded powers and no army. This idea was opposed by Khobe, who held that it would be unwise to disband a body of men who were battle-tested. It was against this backdrop that the UK came to the rescue with IMATT, which paved the way for reforming and building army capacity. Since 1999 strengthening the capacity of the RSLAF has been a central component of Sierra Leone's security sector reform (SSR) process, as well as a key component of the peacebuilding and stabilisation process in the country.

Deployment of UNAMSIL, the largest peacekeeping mission in Africa at the time, brought stability, succour and relief to a people traumatised by war. UNAMSIL maintained a strong military presence; hard-line insurgents finally understood that violence and terror would not be tolerated and national reconciliation of all institutions was under way. The Pakistani Brigade firmly dealt with unrest in Kono, and the 7 Nigerian Battalion ran convoys through Makeni to Kabala and Bumbuna. As part of its objective was to help the national government consolidate its position so as to assume full responsibility for security, UNAMSIL successfully conducted the 2002 proportional general and local elections and stayed in Sierra Leone until the end of 2005. Thus it was the timely intervention of

ECOMOG, UNAMSIL and the UK that ended the bloodshed and restored peace to our beloved motherland.

Transformation of the Armed Forces

Following the restoration of peace in 2002, the need for an effective military machinery became obvious. In particular, the RSLMF has been targeted for restructuring. In January 2002 the new Ministry of Defence (MoD) was opened and the armed forces were officially renamed the RSLAF in recognition of a new start for a new force. At the same time, the defence headquarters ceased to exist and was replaced by two organisations working in parallel, both of which were subordinate to the MoD: the HQ joint force command (JFC) and HQ joint support command (JSC), both under the command of IMATT. The chief of defence staff was just a figurehead; armed forces restructuring was effectively being run by IMATT.

The JFC brought the land, maritime and air components of the RSLAF together under the operational command of the joint force commander, who was responsible for the planning and conduct of all RSLAF operations. RSLAF operations were controlled by IMATT from the JFC headquarters and in Cockerill barracks in Freetown. The task of the JSC has been to establish personnel, administration, logistics, and other organisational requirements to support the RSLAF. Operational readiness and the ability of the armed forces to react quickly and effectively to any incident or threat have depended on the JSC's ability to support the front-line forces, which was achieved by creating a single and unified command structure under IMATT.

The main objective of the MoD within the strategic environment was established: to evaluate threats to national security, political and economic development. The MoD is also tasked to identify relevant formations and units to counter perceived threats to national security and develop appropriate, affordable security policies, programmes and procedures to deal with them. However, the SLPP government began this restructuring process by promoting favouritism and bypassing rules and regulations to ensure that some of its military and civilian supporters (such as Civil Defence Force Kamajors) were put in key positions at the MoD. Those selected and groomed during the APC regime prior to the conflict now served under SLPP political leadership. Professional standards were as prior to the conflict: sidelined for political interests. Some of these civilians were not properly trained or qualified for their appointments. They were given positions of deputy secretary, the equivalent of brigadiers (ten years' service), and senior assistant secretary, the equivalent to colonels (seven years' service). The director general was assessed as a major general. There was no juxtaposition between the director general and the chief of defence staff, with the deputy minister caught in the middle. Inevitably, this created tension at the MoD. There was nothing IMATT could do to counter this political interference; it had inherited a highly politicised military establishment and was faced with the challenge of simultaneously reforming the military while absorbing the implications of the country's culture. By the same token, the Sierra Leone military was learning to understand the culture of IMATT in an effort to build a successful collaboration for reform.

Threat analysis carried out at this time indicated that the majority of security threats to the country were internal, not external, and that the Sierra Leone Police (SLP) should have primacy in addressing internal security issues, with the option of military aid to civil power (MACP). In other words, soldiers would no longer be responsible for internal security. Before the advent of the MACP policy, there was bitter acrimony, misconception and rancour between the SLP and RSLAF, which eventually led to the signing of a memorandum of understanding (MoU) delineating army-police responsibilities. Since the MoU, the division of labour between army and police is much clearer; the relationship much more effective. Soldiers no longer serve at checkpoints; they can only deploy when asked to do so and must return to barracks when ordered. There has been retraining and reorientation of RSLAF staff to accept the doctrines of constitutional supremacy and improvements in the welfare of officers and men, both in service and in retirement.

Financial control and accountability play an important part in the control and accountability of the RSLAF and are now exercised by Parliament through the MoD, with the director general carrying overall responsibility. Funding is tight; except in urgent situations, funding policy means that resources allocated by the government for one purpose should not be reallocated to another without political authorisation.

Within a democratic framework, the RSLAF has to deal with the challenge of transforming itself into a 'user-friendly' organisation. There should be modalities for promoting a mutually beneficial relationship with the national legislature. The importance of the relationship between members of the armed forces and the civilian populace cannot be overemphasised. Until this is internalised and the culture of democracy accepted and institutionalised through systems and behaviour, the armed forces will not be able to adjust to the realities of survival in a democratic system.

Reflections on Civil-Military Relations in Sierra Leone

The military performs its role and tasks in conjunction with other stakeholders, such as government ministers, civil society and the international community. The state provides the purpose, the military the means and the people the will. No military can be effective unless it is founded on sound traditions of discipline, professionalism, bravery and inspirational leadership. It is also a truism that no military operates effectively without civilian partners.

However, instead of advancing on these fundamental truisms, during the 1990s Sierra Leone's armed forces collapsed for a variety of reasons, threw the entire society into anarchy with catastrophic consequences and alienated the RSLAF even further from the population. This led to the development of deep-seated public animosity against the military.

The civilian perspective holds several negative conceptions of the RSLAF. They include the military intervention in politics through a series of coups, the unprofessional attitude of the majority of the military, displayed in particular by soldiers who perceive themselves to be above the law, and the military's inability to stop the atrocities perpetrated by rebels, and in some cases soldiers.

Meanwhile, the military blamed civilian authorities for the strained civil-military relationship and lack of discipline, claiming that politicians interfered in the running of the military, threw professionalism and competence overboard, failed to promote economic development and maintain the rule of law and could or would not improve their conditions of service. The lack of respect for soldiers and the low esteem of the military, along with the creation of the Kamajors as a parallel military force, widened the gap between the army and the population.

The Role of the International Military Assistance Training Team

IMATT provides military advice to the MoD, and the commander of IMATT is the military adviser to the GoSL. The timely intervention of the UK was instrumental in ending the war and establishing a stable, secure environment.

The relevant UK aim for Sierra Leone is to support the government of Sierra Leone in the development of effective, democratically accountable and affordable armed forces, capable of meeting specified defence missions and tasks. IMATT's primary operational role is to train the RSLAF to meet international military standards. IMATT has integrated its officers into the RSLAF chain of command, not simply as advisers but also as serving staff.

The visit of former British Prime Minister Tony Blair and UK government ministers to Sierra Leone in 2007 had an important symbolic purpose: it publicly demonstrated the UK's commitment to Sierra Leone.

The fact that IMATT entered into armed forces reform in Sierra Leone as a neutral force has allowed it to provide objectivity in the management of security matters and issues. Its presence has led to more public confidence in the country's security reform and operations. Even if IMATT did not fully understand the intricacies of the security problems in Sierra Leone initially, its presence acted as a buffer between civil society and the RSLAF, whose relationship had been rife with suspicion and distrust.

From the beginning of the IMATT presence, the people preferred talking to its staff rather than to the military, and public confidence in the potential transformation of the RSLAF into a democratic and accountable institution increased. While IMATT developed an executive role and had the final say about the running of the RSLAF, its most important function was its presence in army staff positions. This positioning of trained, professional officers within the RSLAF chain of command proved to be a vital strategy by which to train Sierra Leonean officers to take over these posts eventually.

The Military Reintegration Programme

Sierra Leone's disarmament, demobilisation and reintegration (DDR) of RUF, AFRC and CDF (Civil Defence Force) combatants began in 2000. The DDR programme had no option but to offer blanket amnesty to all soldiers and officers in June 1999 and invite them to take up arms again. Thus the challenge for DDR became the transformation and integration of ex-combatants coming out of a vicious civil war into a viable and effective fighting machine.

The new armed forces would be composed of former combatants of the Sierra Leone Army, RUF, CDF and the AFRC who had been reintegrated through the DDR programme. This was followed by an intensive refresher course at the Armed Forces Training Centre and a special military reintegration programme for the purpose of integrating all ex-combatants into a single armed force. About 2,500 personnel, 150 of whom were officers, were absorbed into the RSLAF through this programme in 2001/2002.

The DDR screening process was mainly focused on literacy and numeracy. All warring factions were absorbed into the army; some were given command appointments. Promotion was accomplished through appraisal reports; there were no noticeable differences in promotion based on past allegiances. Many ex-combatants were sent to take training courses in Ghana, where some failed woefully. Their problems were compounded when they became the first casualties of the downsizing phase for officers.

The British training programme began in the year 2000, partly as an exit strategy for UNAMSIL peacekeepers. In June 2000 a team of 200 trainers drawn from the Second Royal Anglican Regiment of the British Army arrived in Freetown to begin a training programme named Operation Basilica. Located at the Benguema training centre, this six-week programme trained 1,000 recruits. At the same time, 40 army captains attended a retraining course sponsored by the UK government at the Ghana staff college. The second phase of the training programme, funded by £20 million (approximately US$35 million) of UK funds, facilitated the training and retraining of 8,500 officers and soldiers required for the new army. So far, rightsizing the RSLAF has been carried out in phases: phase one in January 2004 retired 784 personnel, phase two in January 2005 retired 1,000 personnel and phase three in January 2006 retired 1,092 personnel.

Many of the 1999 officer intake have since been trained through IMATT's Operation Silkman, attending the UK short-term training team's platoon commanders' battle course. In the main, this was the group recruited by the SLPP to be the 'New Army'. IMATT personnel were tempted to turn to these officers as the best chance of consolidating reform efforts to wash away the stains left by their predecessors, believing the new officers had the flexibility, open-mindedness and idealism of young officers everywhere. However, these new officers viewed senior officers with contempt, as they mistakenly believed their only reason for joining the army was to rid it of the legacy of such officers. The true picture of officer competency was more complex: some senior officers had distinguished themselves, not only in Africa but far beyond. Many were highly principled and had acted accordingly (then as now), but they were the exceptions and had often been marginalised by previous governments.

RSLAF officers worked side by side with IMATT, learning at all levels of the military hierarchy and leading eventually to a command review.

The review illustrated the need to abolish the JSC and establish the assistant chief of defence staff, personnel and training in parallel to the already existing systems for operations and plans and support and logistics. The review also emphasised the dire need for downsizing and clarifying roles between civilians and military, IMATT and the RSLAF. IMATT relinquished most executive roles and returned to advising and mentoring, thus accommodating the need for local ownership.

Achievements and Lessons Learned: Restructuring Sierra Leone's Armed Forces

One aspect of restructuring the security sector is the process whereby an oversized army is reduced in phases to a new structure. Without the restructuring programme, there would have been no financial headroom for future improvements. Restructuring has had a major positive impact on RSLAF in the long term; the new structure continues to provide a significant number of promotions spread across the whole restructuring period. It is easy to be negative about how the process has occurred, but the overriding objective is to ensure that restructuring is conducted in a positive way and the RSLAF avoids stagnation and getting involved in unconstitutional activities such as coups d'état. All parties involved envisioned a smaller, more capable, professional and better-equipped force enjoying an enhanced package of terms and conditions of service. Such an achievement could not have been realised without the full support and cooperation of all formations and commanders.

The downsizing process: Who was involved?

The Defence Council agreed on the future shape and size of the RSLAF. In purely numerical terms, the force figure of 15,500 troops was reduced to 10,500 by December 2006. This reduction in numbers was achieved gradually; the first phase occurred in January 2004.

In the second downsizing phase in 2005, the resettlement target was 1,000 personnel; their past allegiances were not deemed relevant. However, only those with ten or more years' service received a resettlement pension; a financial package was offered to those with less than ten years' service. Officers were not involved at this stage, as there was already a deficit of over 300. Since there was also a shortage in most specialist trades, they were not included in this second downsizing phase.

The net loss in the order of battle was only two infantry battalions (1,086 posts) towards the end of the restructuring process. However, those selected for resettlement were not necessarily from those two battalions, but were to be taken from across the whole RSLAF infantry. The downsizing process emphasised the importance of providing clear and comprehensive information not only to the RSLAF but also to the public about all aspects, including the reasons for troop reduction and its implications. IMATT briefings throughout the RSLAF chain of command about the details and implications of downsizing proved invaluable.

The restructuring process – Ongoing needs

The process of re-establishing, restructuring and retraining the RSLAF began in earnest in 2000. If past mistakes are not to be repeated, avoiding those things that went wrong with the RSLAF in the past must be deemed of the highest importance.

By 1967 serious distortions had occurred in the structure of the armed forces. In addition, some military officials found themselves being used to resolve the unsettled political succession problem during this period. This laid the foundation for direct interference by politicians in pure military matters; the armed forces were drawn into mainstream politics and politicking.

The result of this politicisation has been that the armed forces today contain officers who did not meet the standard requirements for recruitment and those who had been promoted beyond their qualifications on the basis of political considerations. Others had key roles in the overthrow of democratically elected governments or had committed gross human rights violations during the war years.

Therefore, while much has been done, there is a need for vigorous rescreening and restructuring of the RSLAF in order to facilitate fully the restoration of discipline and professionalism. All officers who were recruited without meeting the standard requirements should be released from service. Besides removing undesirable personnel from the army, such an exercise would drive home the message of professionalism within the RSLAF.

It is also necessary to continue to restore dignity, social prestige and service pride to armed forces members. An important step is to address the problem of ordnance, particularly uniform items. A soldier's turnout matters a great deal to him and constitutes a major factor in how he is perceived by the wider society. New RSLAF personnel should be issued with uniforms, kit and equipment to meet their basic administrative and operational needs. Battle and support equipment must not only be of high quality, but must be procured with due regard to the capabilities required, roles to be undertaken and funding limitations. The Defence Tenders Board should endorse requirements and specifications prior to orders being placed. Tender and procurement processes must be competitive and transparent.

Another critical concern is the need for retraining and reorientation of personnel in order to keep the military out of politics and prepare them to be able to perform their military tasks. Within a democratic society, armed forces should be trained, controlled, equipped and deployed in such a way that they are robust enough to act as an effective deterrent to groups who might resort to armed violence. Throughout the years of restructuring and reform under discussion here, Sierra Leone has witnessed the continued, low-lying threat of the return of armed violence and conflict; the military still needs to be aware of the potential to relapse into conflict.

The international community should assist the government in equipping and modernising the RSLAF through provision of modern arms, barracks, uniforms, communication equipment and vehicles. Parallel to specific RSLAF issues, the wider society should encourage the promotion of a culture of merit, fairness and high standards. The best way to do this is by developing a political environment which insulates military personnel from direct contact with politicians and a bureaucracy that operates outside the military chain of command.

The RSLAF should also carry out a programme of internal education among its personnel so as to limit their expectations. It is vital that RSLAF soldiers understand that the country's resources have been depleted by the war; the military has to compete for scarce resources like other segments of society and may have to operate with a great deal of improvisation. The wider society, especially political opponents of the government, should not seek to interpret the government's inability to provide all that is needed as unwillingness or lack of interest in the military by the ruling political party. In other words, all political actors, both internal and external, should send clear signals to soldiers that the wider society expects them to make sacrifices, perform their functions according to their constitutional duty, obey the incumbent government and make the best use of what is available.

However, beyond this initial training programme, it is important to institute and fund a comprehensive programme for continuous RSLAF training. For example, some of the vehicles essential for meaningful training are presently in dire need of spares and basic equipment. Similarly, institutional facilities are needed to undertake even the most elementary and fundamental training. Since the inception of the RSLMF in 1961, the army has not had even a junior staff college, let alone a senior division. Having helped us with the building of the Horton Academy, IMATT should now organise and provide staff for junior division staff course training from 2009 onward.

Efforts should also be intensified to identify and confirm offers of additional staff training from other countries worldwide. Such offers must be considered as part of an overall training strategy managed by the MoD. Without such outside support, the organisational reforms and capacity required to establish sustainable and accountable armed forces under effective civil control may not be achieved. Training in other countries assists the RSLAF to assess its own standards, acquire new techniques and broaden the outlook of the participating personnel. This also serves as an incentive for the rest of the armed forces to work hard and adhere to high professional standards and loyalty. In turn, training in other countries has a stabilising effect on the military command structure, as it provides for the most capable officers to rise to leadership positions. Officers who gain leadership posts under this system are less likely to plot coups or participate in partisan politics.

Support to killed and wounded in action

Restructuring activities have included payments for personnel killed in action (KIA), wounded in action (WIA) and dying naturally: 3,029 beneficiaries were paid in 2004 for personnel KIA. In phase one of WIA, 290 personnel were paid terminal and disability benefits in 2005, while in phase two 345 personnel were screened and certified as medically disabled. The latter are still awaiting payment. IMATT and DFID have been instrumental in the handling of KIA payments and WIA support; in a country in dire economic straits, non-payment of KIA and WIA would have led to obvious security concerns.

Due to the nature of injuries sustained by combatants during the war, it is difficult, and in some cases impossible, for a number of discharged WIA to find employment. During the restructuring process, it was agreed that WIA would be further assessed to ascertain the level and percentage of disability in order to decide on an enhanced benefit payment over and above what they were entitled to under their terms of service. A technical committee was formed to establish a formula to allow fair and equitable payment to WIA personnel qualifying for disability pensions. The proposal was forwarded to the chief of defence staff that an individual's salary should continue to be his monthly pension. Conscious of the fact that those KIA paid the supreme price, a KIA committee was also formed to ensure that they did not die in vain and families left behind receive benefits. A verification exercise was designed to curb possible fraudsters.

A total of 1,466 beneficiaries were entitled to payments of benefits due to natural deaths of RSLAF personnel. This is causing a major challenge for both the RSLAF and the government, and has significant security implications. Most dependants continue to occupy quarters which are needed by serving personnel. It is, however, unfair for them to be told to hand over their quarters when benefits have not been paid yet.

Improving the welfare of officers and men

Improving the welfare and living conditions of current and ex-servicemen would address the need to ensure that the military stays out of politics. At the moment, most of the defence estate is in a dilapidated state. Except for the newly constructed barracks produced through Operation Pebu and the rehabilitated Teko Barracks, virtually no substantial maintenance has been conducted for the past ten years. Furthermore, the recent conflict inflicted serious damage on many buildings, with the result that water supply, latrines, sewage disposal and electrical wiring are now highly inadequate. It must also be noted that the strength of the army was less than 3,000 men at the onset of the war, but eventually rose to over 15,500, with major consequences for accommodation.

Thus a major practical step is to accommodate all RSLAF personnel in barracks built to acceptable standards. If the current unsatisfactory arrangement is not addressed, it could lead to disaffection and lack of discipline. Single personnel should be accommodated in barracks and not, as is currently standard, be required to find accommodation in the local community. Additional married quarters are also required. This will minimise RSLAF interaction with wider society and undue exposure to socio-political pressure. Most importantly, such an arrangement will assist the military leadership in monitoring its personnel, restoring the traditions and values of the military profession and facilitating preventive measures to counter any attempt to mobilise troops for a coup. On the other hand, when soldiers are too isolated from the general population, this can lead to misunderstanding and mistrust. Some integration and community interaction should be encouraged.

Apart from accommodation, living standards of RSLAF personnel need to be significantly improved. Among the lower ranks, poverty and economic insecurity have been cited as factors that encourage military involvement in politics. It is necessary to ensure that military personnel and their families are given middle-class living conditions and assistance to buy modest houses upon retirement, as part of the National Social Security and Insurance Trust programme.

There should be adequate capability available to ensure that personnel are fit and ready to carry out clear and defined instruction, thus discouraging the habit of leaving their duty posts unnecessarily. The current situation makes regimental administration difficult, if not impossible. At times rice is available but with no condiments, and ration cash allowances are often paid late. Similarly, most formation and unit troop-carrying vehicles are unserviceable due to the non-availability of tyres, oil, air and fuel filters to conduct routine servicing. Thus, transport capability at tactical level is slowly grinding to a halt.

A comprehensive post-service programme for effective reintegration into civil society is also imperative for Sierra Leone's future stability. By the nature of the military profession, some of the most vital skills developed within the RSLAF are not utilised in the civil sector. This is particularly true for the infantry, which constitute the bulk of the military. The most common civilian job available for this category on retirement is that of security guard, where wage structure and conditions of service are unbefitting rewards for their distinguished service. This cannot be reconciled to the skill level and lifestyle they have acquired in service. Former soldiers who seek to avoid undergoing this humiliating experience may be tempted to acts of corruption or crime, or succumb to material inducements and promises from individuals pursuing their own political and economic interests. A programme must thus be introduced to enable soldiers to acquire skills for post-service life and engage honourably in a civilian capacity. Coupled with good governance, transparency, leadership by example and political will, this would help to keep soldiers out of coup planning.

Welfare requirements of the armed forces are multidimensional and demand urgent attention. However, considering the limited resources available to both the government and the armed forces, these demands need to be addressed in order of priority. The five major priority areas on which the limited resources should be focused are:

- Operational imperatives must take priority over welfare and estate
- Provision of barracks accommodation for all soldiers
- Provision of basic amenities and conveniences necessary to make such accommodation habitable by soldiers and their families
- Pay review and increased salaries and allowances for soldiers
- Introduction of a comprehensive post-service programme to enable ex-soldiers to reintegrate properly into civil society

These five priority areas, if addressed effectively, will go a long way to discourage officers and men from the temptations of intervention in politics and governance.

Operation Pebu

Operation Pebu has been ongoing since March 2003. The original idea was to tackle the RSLAF's accommodation needs up-country as an interim measure between the disarmament of combatants and the consolidation of the new RSLAF in battalion sites. The initial plan involved construction at seven sites: Simbakoro, Moyamba, Yele, Kambia, Kabala, Pujehun and Kailahun. Office and technical accommodation was provided first and was completed by mid-2003, when the original form of the project was suspended. Domestic accommodation was the second priority; the work restarted at Pujehun and Kailahun in April 2005 after a number of delays in building according to the original design.

The initial costing of generic modern barracks, with a proper road network, complete electrical and plumbing systems and all ancillary structures, ranging from schools to a marketplace, was considered unaffordable at US$7 million for each site. The aim for Operation Pebu – domestic accommodation – was to maximise the number of units that could be provided with funds available. Consequently, accommodation was designed at the most basic level to last three to five years until the future structure of the RSLAF could be determined. The assumption was that the size of the RSLAF would be reduced over time, and a programme of permanent building would begin to replace the temporary Operation Pebu housing.

Originally there were two principal stakeholders, DFID and the GoSL, both of which contributed funding and manpower: around Le2.33 billion (approximately US$0.77 million) and Le2.45 billion (approximately US$0.8 million), respectively, per barrack. The barracks in Kailahun, Simbakoro and Kabala were funded by the GoSL; those at Moyamba, Pujehun, Yele and

Kambia by DFID. The project evolved over time, so that there are now three principal stakeholders: DFID, IMATT, RSLAF/GoSL. The RSLAF and the government funded timber and corrugated iron; DFID and IMATT funded cement, aggregate and sand. The latter were supplied on 'call off' contract, i.e. the project manager is required to instruct the contractor when deliveries will be required, but the invoices are sent directly to DFID for payment.

The original (2003) project manager structure had a five-member steering committee based at the MoD. Subordinate to that was an IMATT project management team headed by a UK lieutenant colonel. After commencement of the project, it became quite obvious that the ambitious completion date of May 2004 was unachievable. The experiences acquired during implementation of Operation Pebu have warranted a rethink of the concept, leading to revised calculations based on troop production capacity and availability and level of construction supervision. In order to increase RSLAF ownership and capacity, a chief officer from the Engineer Regiment was appointed as project manager in April 2006; IMATT (and to some extent the steering committee) ceded some of their managing role to this officer. Operation Pebu project sites at Kailahun and Pujehun are ongoing; when completed, they will house approximately 350 soldiers and their families.[2]

In a related developmental project, IMATT funded the refurbishment of married quarters at Teko Barracks in Makeni. The work has been carried out expeditiously and to a high standard by 4 Brigade with IMATT mentoring. IMATT has provided Le200.6 million (approximately US$66,000), which has enabled the refurbishment of 90 blocks of six married quarters each, housing 540 families.

National security architecture

A very important development in addressing security challenges in Sierra Leone was the creation of the national security architecture (NSA), which coordinates the implementation of all security matters. The NSA consists of three key strategic forums: the National Security Council (NSC), the National Security Council Coordinating Group (NSCCG) and the Office of National Security (ONS). The NSCCG is the forum for heads of primary security institutions and senior public officials from key line ministries. It provides security direction on policies, priorities and objectives to the security sector and intelligence agencies. It also coordinates and monitors the activities of the provincial security committees (PROSECs) and district security committees (DISECs).

Through the community, DISECs provide feedback mechanisms to the NSA, thus allowing citizens to participate in the governance of their security by engaging in discussion of early warning signals indicating threats to state security. The RSLAF plays an important role in all activities of the ONS, NSC, NSCCG, PROSECs, DISECs, Joint Intelligence Committee and HQ operational command to prevent and respond to external and internal security threats.

Training and recruitment

Training and retraining are essential ingredients in the rebirth of the military as an institution of national pride and integration. The vision of the personnel and training branch is to ensure professional, highly motivated personnel and training services manned, developed and configured to deliver, within budget, the highest quality of services.

Training facilities at Benguema and Horton Academy[3] have been upgraded. Current training is intended to build the capacity of the RSLAF to carry out its constitutional responsibility effectively. There have also been moves made to improve internal opportunities to further academic education up to the PhD level, with the aim of recruiting more graduates into the army.

With the assistance of donor partners, including IMATT, UK, USA, China, Mali, ECOWAS, Kofi Annan International Peacekeeping Training Centre, Greece, Ghana, Nigeria and Egypt, many overseas military training activities have been taking place.

On the educational front, the RSLAF has launched a literacy and numeracy project to build on the training already delivered by the Armed Forces Education Centre. By increasing the output of such training, it is hoped to develop standards significantly within the RSLAF and increase the number of soldiers benefiting from attendance. To date, 3,400 RSLAF personnel at various levels have been trained. AFEC, in conjunction with Partners in Adult Education Coordinating Office, recruited more civilian teachers to conduct literacy training nationwide for the RSLAF. This is carried out with active IMATT financial support.

The RSLAF is also aware that delivery of high-quality care at military medical centres is hampered by current difficulties faced by the Defence Medical Services. With the help of IMATT, medical staff have been able to undertake refresher training, a number of medical nurses have upgraded their skills and other specialists have qualified as state enrolled community health nurses.

Operations

RSLAF experience in military operations dates back to the First World War. In the past two decades the country has participated in many operations: suppressing internal insurrection, low-intensity conflicts and international operations in support of Mano River Union, ECOWAS and UN mandates. In spite of this experience, noticeable areas of difficulties often hampered performance in these operations. To meet international standards, adequate training and preparations, including logistics and equipment, for personnel in all military operations are required.

Military operations are still an evolving concept. Our experiences in various operations have not been properly documented and the lessons learnt are yet to be studied to enable the country to evolve its own doctrine. The peculiarities of peace support operations (PSO) in Africa have also opened up new areas of intellectual research, and these experiences would help provide the framework for the doctrine of RSLAF operations, including PSO training.

The RSLAF, women and security

In October 2000 UN Security Council Resolution 1325 proposed a framework to address women's security issues at local, regional and international levels. It recommends that the UN Security Council, UN member states and civil society should endeavour to address four important issues: the need for the participation of women in all decision-making and peace processes in conflict states; the importance of integrating gender perspectives in training for peacekeeping operations; the obligation to protect women from gender-based violence in conflict zones; and the need to mainstream gender into UN reporting systems and programme implementation mechanisms.

The effect of the Sierra Leone conflict on women was devastating. More than a third of the population were displaced and lived in camps, or had fled to other locations. The fighting increased the overall burden placed on women. During the war women did not join the armed forces in any number, but since the end of the war the military has made significant progress to ensure the inclusion of women.

There have been a number of policy adjustments regarding recruitment, training and retention of women in the RSLAF; through the use of quotas, we have achieved a significant increase in women's participation in the military. While we have maintained the academic criteria necessary to recruit suitable personnel, recruitment base standards (including physical fitness) have been restructured to accommodate more women. Dialogue, discussions, seminars and workshops with women's advocacy groups have been encouraged to create awareness in our female soldiers. Opening up the institution to women is enhancing better civil-military relations.

Efforts have also been made to attract qualified women to leadership roles in order to participate actively in decision-making at higher command levels. (The highest-ranking woman in the RSLAF currently is a colonel.) However, while many mechanisms have been put in place to monitor problems based on gender issues, sexual harassment policies for the RSLAF need to be established.

The RSLAF military justice system

During the 1970s the right to appeal charges of treason was quashed. Under the 1990s' regime, soldiers and officers were charged through 'summary dealings', popularly known as 'orders'. There was no right of appeal except through a body called 'prerogative of mercy'. The RSLAF Act of 1961 (as amended) set out the categories of military offences. Violation of these offences may have led to the accused being charged. Before then there had been no framework that could be called the legal branch. The most important development that has taken place in the legal branch during the period under scrutiny here is the reintroduction of a military criminal court system and a court martial system.

A building at the JFC headquarters at Cockerill now serves as the court martial centre. In the absence of adequate professional staff to run the court, IMATT recruited two civilian lawyers who are currently serving in the positions of prosecutor and defence counsel for a period of two years. It is expected that by the end of their contracts the army will have its own lawyers, since there are presently four captains in different stages of training at the University of Sierra Leone, sponsored by an IMATT scholarship scheme.

IMATT and MoD/RSLAF relations

The present relationship between IMATT and the RSLAF can be described as cordial, professional, friendly and effective. IMATT operates with an ethos characterised by partnership, respect, transparency and flexibility; the RSLAF has responded in a similar fashion, thus ensuring that a strong partnership is maintained. The RSLAF has benefited in particular from IMATT training in the critical activity of planning, with an eye to eventual fiscal sustainability of the military by the GoSL.

The only area of great concern in the IMATT-RSLAF relationship was the initial planning of Operation Pebu, where RSLAF views were not considered. There have been claims and counter-claims by IMATT and the RSLAF about the success and failures of Operation Pebu and other building projects. The RSLAF claims that if IMATT had listened to its views, they could have concentrated on building modern barracks on just three battalion sites with DFID financial support. In turn, the government's own contribution could have been used to build the capacity of the army in terms of equipment and fuel procurement. The RSLAF would have preferred building army accommodation similar to that constructed by DFID for the SLP.

IMATT itself has countered that the RSLAF should also shoulder responsibility for Operation Pebu, as the RSLAF established programme management, yardsticks and timelines, all of which led to low-quality construction and even theft from construction sites. It is my view that Operation Pebu was a flawed concept. It was first framed as a temporary measure, but exhibited conflicting expectations between the RSLAF and IMATT. However, we should not be overly mesmerised by the mixed success of Operation Pebu and allow it to overshadow IMATT's overall success.

IMATT holds the view that with training and the right influences, new officer recruits could become commanders who would match the quality of officers that exists elsewhere in West Africa. These recruits are a bright, ambitious and restless group; it is understandable that IMATT would consider them to be the best vehicle for RSLAF reform. IMATT believes that these young men are in a hurry, and impatience could easily turn to frustration and action. IMATT is optimistic that this group will be the first to command the RSLAF competently without foreign 'guidance' or 'hand-holding'.

Although members of both the RSLAF and IMATT are positively disposed to the core review, especially the reduction of the RSLAF to 8,500, some members of the RSLAF are concerned that downsizing without corresponding force multipliers will leave the army with less capacity.

In the initial stages of IMATT's presence in Sierra Leone it held executive appointments at the MoD, JFC and JSC. IMATT gradually handed back these executive appointments, except for chief of operations at the JFC and director of intelligence and security at the MoD. Short-term training teams also assisted in resuscitating the RSLAF following the conflict by conducting battalion-level collective and special arms training. IMATT helped in re-establishing and building civil-military relations by conducting post-war confidence patrols with the RSLAF and funding some civil-military cooperation projects.

IMATT is a bold experiment and an innovative strategic concept. Over time, it has changed markedly from an executive to an advisory agency. It is a concrete manifestation of the UK commitment to establish a serious long-term partnership with Sierra Leone to address the issues that present challenges to our mutual security interest in this new century.

Command Autonomy

There will always be a temptation for power players to seek support from elements in the military to enhance their political objectives by appealing to ethnic solidarity, economic difficulties, social disharmony, religion, etc. Such appeals might not be overt and, accordingly, may escape the immediate attention of the intelligence community. It is therefore the task of the military leadership to maintain professionalism and monitor formal and informal relationships.

There has to be the political will and consensus in the wider society to discourage the reintroduction of politics within the armed forces. It should be the norm for our elite to avoid intrusion into the recruitment, promotion, training and appointment processes of the armed forces. Once clear policy and guidelines have been established, they should be allowed to run their natural course within the military command structure. There should be no covert or subtle efforts to bend accepted rules and regulations governing these processes in favour of particular individuals. The military leadership should be given the autonomy to implement policies laid down by the government and enforce rules and regulations without undue pressure.

If abuses occur, let them be corrected and managed within the military command structure. Military personnel with one foot in the armed forces and the other in political circles should be exposed and barred from leadership positions.

We must stop promoting and rewarding people according to time served, and start demanding performance. All good militaries separate the wheat from the chaff, and so must we. Integrity is the most important attribute of a military officer.

The RSLAF has welcomed the role of IMATT in reforming and building the capacity of Sierra Leone's army, and would like to see a skeletal IMATT staff remain even after its final official withdrawal. With IMATT's continued presence on the ground, it will continue to promote objectivity and transparency and attract funding based on realism.

The Present Image of the RSLAF

The MoD and RSLAF are now instruments capable of serving the public good and providing aid and protection to their citizens. The MoD's institutional capacity is sufficient to undertake its responsibility to direct, manage and ensure RSLAF accountability, improve the management of fixed assets and provide better-trained civilian and military staff.

Due to their recent horrible experience, a cross-section of Sierra Leoneans now believe and espouse the view that there is 'no sustainable development without security'. If serious and sustainable measures are not taken to build and maintain a strong national security apparatus, then the nation's vision of a peaceful, prosperous and progressive society will remain an empty dream. Most Sierra Leoneans are appreciative of the government's security reforms, reflected in the ongoing reform of the military and police, and the creation of the ONS and other such institutions. However, more needs to be done to build, consolidate and sustain the national security apparatus. In particular, the country needs modern, well-trained and equipped, highly motivated and dependable security forces imbued with professional values.

The new RSLAF is a credible, non-partisan, well-trained fighting force. The peaceful, legitimate and fair elections that took place in August/September 2007 indicated the return of stability. Territorial integrity is being maintained by the RSLAF within the bounds of MACP; the RSLAF is strategically deployed throughout the country, enabling internally displaced people and refugees to return safely to their homes and families.

In conjunction with the SLP, the RSLAF is fulfilling its role in the existing NSA and continues to provide the enabling, peaceful and conducive environment necessary to guarantee sustainable development. In the 2007 elections the RSLAF supported the SLP within the MACP framework by pre-positioning troops before, during and after the elections to respond to the threat of conflict. It also provided troops for joint mobile patrols with the SLP before the run-off elections when tensions were high. Considering the restive agitation of the masses, the SLP could not have done it alone; when the SLP requested its assistance, the RSLAF played an essential role in ensuring a peaceful election process.

After years of wrenching conflict that tore Sierra Leone apart, the progress made in the restructuring and modernisation of the country's armed forces is gratifying.

Future Challenges

The next decade (2010–2019) could pose both political and military challenges to the RSLAF, due to its front-line role in safeguarding the territorial integrity of the country and its quest to participate in UN, AU and ECOWAS peacekeeping missions. The characteristics of the environment in which the RSLAF will operate in the next decade dictate that its forces should continue to be restructured. While globalisation is turning the world into one village, our force deployment could be limited to West Africa. Today, local or internal conflicts in one state are easily internationalised by global media coverage and can quickly draw in other nations. Our nation thus needs to re-evaluate its force structure to ensure that we meet the geo-strategic challenges of our immediate environment.

The challenge is to design a national defence programme that will deliver capable armed forces within the limits of national resources. This involves long-term planning in every aspect of defence to enhance RSLAF capabilities. By making difficult choices and trade-offs, the nation will be able to preserve the core capabilities and flexibility necessary to meet Sierra Leone's security needs. It is therefore prudent for IMATT to leave a skeleton staff after the end of its mandate, to assist the RSLAF with this long-term planning in achieving its defence missions and military tasks.

The RSLAF has considered the following reasons why it needs longer-term IMATT assistance.

National interests and objectives. With a land border of over 3,000 kilometres, Sierra Leone needs a military capable of blunting enemy action along the borders. One objective is to deter any aggression that could threaten the nation's security and, when deterrence fails, repel or defeat military attacks. The RSLAF requires access to force multipliers to accomplish its national objectives. IMATT could advise the GoSL in the future on the issue of modern force multipliers.

National strategy. The RSLAF needs to be trained in PSO participation, which requires specialist training skills. IMATT could establish a PSO training centre in conjunction with the UN.

National military strategy. The RSLAF does not have any defined military doctrine for achieving its defence missions and military tasks. IMATT needs to advise and assist the RSLAF in designing a national military strategy.

Allies. One factor which states cannot afford to ignore when structuring their forces is the alliance system. Most documents regulating relations among allies include clauses that can make mandatory intervention on the side of the attacked member state. Thus the structuring of the RSLAF cannot ignore the French factor (its alliance with Guinea), even if all the nation may need to do is to seek a counterbalance elsewhere, such as with the UK.

Technology. Technological advancement has altered the nature of war. Continued technological modernisation of the RSLAF would enable it to cope better with the realities of the modern battlefield.

Resource constraints. The performance of a nation's economy directly influences the structure of its forces. There are, however, never enough resources to satisfy all the nation's wants; hence the need to establish requirements, set priorities, make decisions and allocate resources to the most critical. What resource constraints dictate in force structure is the need to arrive at a better-informed judgement concerning the level and mix of the armed forces required. The structure of the RSLAF must consider the possibilities of revenue generation during peacetime, such as through the use of army engineers in civil construction works.

Available forces. At present, Sierra Leone has no formal ally, no prospective plans for mobilisation and no articulated reserve system. This implies it would rely on the forces in active service to cope with immediate challenges until such time that new entrants can be trained and deployed. Therefore, the proposed structure for the RSLAF should articulate a reserve force policy.

Assessment of forces. Force assessment seeks to consider what needs to be done (objectives), how it is to be done (strategy), what the state is up against (threats) and what is available (resources). The variables employed in the comparative analysis of forces are qualitative (leadership, doctrine, training, morale, logistics, intelligence, technology and initiative) and quantitative (order of battle, fire power, mobility, survivability, accuracy, range and weapons effects). Hence a structure is needed which would enable an annual assessment of the RSLAF through joint exercises.

Threat. When there is a strong perception of threat to the security of a nation, there is likely to be a willingness to forgo other needs to prioritise development of a credible force to respond to the threat. The same cannot be said for a nation that is in a state of relative peace. Sierra Leone's contiguous neighbours are Liberia and Guinea. Liberia at the moment cannot police its borders effectively; the continuous occupation of Yenga by Guinean armed forces must be of serious concern to the government of Sierra Leone and the international community, particularly ECOWAS. By occupying Yenga, Guinea might continue to pose threats to the sovereignty of Sierra Leone. In assessing these threats, Sierra Leone must consider conflicts of interest, contiguity, capability, credibility, intentions, circumstances and vulnerabilities. When these aspects are analysed with respect to Sierra Leone's neighbours and its quest to contribute peacekeeping troops, it would be risky to conclude that the country should downsize its armed forces without force multipliers.

Conclusion

Military intervention in politics and governance has undermined Sierra Leone's democratic development. The RSLAF has suffered from a serious decline in discipline and professionalism. As recent Sierra Leone history attests, members of the armed forces compromised allegiance to the state in their collaboration with partisan interests; the coherence of the military and its fighting capability were gravely undermined. Furthermore, as relations between members of the armed forces and their civilian compatriots deteriorated, the military lost the public support it needed to perform its duty to defend the country's territorial integrity.

Since 1999 RSLAF reform, restructuring and capacity-building have been central components of Sierra Leone's SSR process and a key component in peacebuilding and stabilisation. ECOMOG, UNAMSIL and IMATT all played crucial roles in ending the war; IMATT played a subsequent role advising and mentoring the military restructuring process. DDR was an attempt to integrate ex-combatants into a single armed force; it has occurred through the deployment of both UNAMSIL and IMATT, reintegration of combatants into the armed forces, KIA/WIA support and Operation Pebu.

At the same time, the MoD and RSLAF have experienced a significant decline, in real terms, of their budgetary allocations. Consequently, the preparation of security institution strategic and financial plans has become somewhat of an academic exercise because most of what is normally included in such plans is not achieved at the end of the year. For instance, the aspiration to have a viable air wing as a component of the RSLAF is for now a distant dream, while the maritime wing is grossly underfunded. Military estates require significant improvement and investment if service personnel across the country are to live in standard accommodation. But for the donated vehicles from various friendly governments, it is difficult to move personnel and essential supplies to locations where they are required. However, even these highly valued gifts are now becoming difficult to manage, as both running and maintenance costs are having a telling effect on the lean budget.

Defence is an expensive but necessary business. Its requirements stem from the need to protect national assets and interests from internal and external threats. After all, the main causes of the RUF war emanated specifically from the plundering of our essential marine, mineral and agricultural resources. The 1991 RUF insurgency, which escalated into the Sierra Leonean civil war, started as a cross-border incursion by rebels and their accomplices operating from bases in Liberia. For the duration of the war, the rebel movement was constantly reinforced by supplies from across the border. It is widely known that the weakest points in our national security are the porous borders (both land and sea). Over the years this has made it relatively easy for foreigners of all nationalities to walk or sail in and out of the country. They have habitually smuggled out our diamonds, gold, cash and food crops and poached fish from our rivers and sea. Even more horrible was the relative ease with which hoodlums and rebels entered under the guise of liberating the people, only to engage in mass murder, looting and destruction.

In post-conflict Sierra Leone, an integral part of our national security vision must be to protect and police our borders vigorously against all intruders, smugglers, poachers and saboteurs. In the past we have not been particularly good at protecting our assets. The reasons for this are complex, but lie in many years of injustice, bad governance, corruption and mismanagement. If we are to ensure that history does not repeat itself, we need to have loyal, strong, reformed, capable, well-motivated and equipped forces that answer to a democratically elected civilian government.

The present APC government has inherited a number of problems and recognises the contribution that the RSLAF can make to support civil authorities with wide-ranging tasks within MACP, such as reconstruction, rehabilitation and joint off-shore patrols to arrest potential offenders. But funding is tight and the economy is currently 70 per cent financed by international donor agencies. Our soldiers are living in deplorable conditions, some of the worst in the world. The core review, which will lead to rightsizing, is a welcome development, but should be compensated with corresponding force multipliers and equipment modernisation. Efficient army engineers and agricultural units for income generation are also needed. Similarly, planning joint exercises to assess the state of combat readiness in the RSLAF are needed. Conscious effort must be made to train and enable the RSLAF to protect the economic resources of the nation, participate in PSO and aid the government in non-combat roles.

The question is how long our dependence on foreign aid will last. Currently Sierra Leone receives about 40 per cent of the UK's Africa Conflict Prevention Pool. If the complete picture of all IMATT/RSLAF programme funding is considered, IMATT has contributed 50–70 per cent of the RSLAF's budget. This is not easy for hard-working taxpayers in the UK to understand. But while we realise that the UK spends a disproportionate part of its ACPP aid budget in Sierra Leone, it is a fact that the RSLAF needs more. We also realise that the International Monetary Fund and the World Bank are not disposed to fund or support any military spending in the near future; in fact, they frown upon it. The point is that the patience and support of donors are running out. It would be unwise to expect substantial support long after 2012.

The underlying vision of the RSLAF is for a nation that institutes an effective government devoid of corruption and offers Sierra Leoneans an improved quality of life through economic progress and prosperity in a safe and secure environment. This is what the RSLAF is working to achieve in difficult circumstances.

Notes

1 Kamajors refer to traditional hunters in Sierra Leone, many of whom joined the Civil Defence Force (CDF). The CDF supported the government of Sierra Leone against the Revolutionary United Front (RUF), and were led by Samuel Hinga Norman.

2 Operation Pebu was, in October 2008, finalised in Kailahun and Pujehun.

3 Over the reporting period of 2002–2007, the Armed Forces Training Centre has turned out an estimated 210 second lieutenants and 940 young soldiers, at an annual rate of 30 officer cadets and 120 recruits. It has regularly conducted career courses for young officers, junior and senior non-commissioned officers on an annual basis. These courses cover professional and career training, including platoon commander battle courses, platoon sergeant battle courses, and section commander battle and combatant team commander courses. Over the period, the Horton Academy has conducted continuing professional development courses for officers to enable them to take over any battalion/brigade staff and command positions commensurate to their ranks. The Horton Academy provides officers with basic understanding of the complexities of a PSO environment.

Chapter 9

Formulating Sierra Leone's Defence White Paper

Al-Hassan Kharamoh Kondeh

Introduction

This chapter outlines the process of producing Sierra Leone's 2002 defence white paper. Unique to this process was the document's explicit aim of explaining *to the general public* both the progress and the shortcomings of security sector reform (SSR) in Sierra Leone's defence system. The white paper was produced on the assumption that without making this information publicly available, opportunities to engage ordinary people in future reform initiatives would be limited.

The chapter also describes some of the challenges faced in the white paper's production, including those from military counterparts in the Republic of Sierra Leone Armed Forces (RSLAF) and from international military and civilian advisers.

After a complex process of consultation and debate, the defence white paper is a strong statement of where Sierra Leone's defence sector stands today and the direction it should take in the future. It is obvious that all this chapter's recommendations will not necessarily be implemented in practice. It is also clear that while Sierra Leone has come a long way in building up a strong and democratically accountable defence system, there are still many challenges ahead.

Background

For several decades the military in Sierra Leone was run on an *ad hoc* basis. Its purpose was regime preservation and personal security for politicians. The military was run as a more or less secret cult with little or no accountability to the public or any form of oversight mechanisms in place. In particular, senior officers displayed little concern for the people whom they were supposed to serve. Indeed, the people, as well as state institutions, were not taken into consideration at all by the military/political regime. Loyalty of the military rested upon the political class that guaranteed them promotion and job security. This situation, prolonged over a period of years, contributed to the total collapse of security throughout the country. By 1991, when the Revolutionary United Front (RUF) unleashed its terror on Sierra Leone, the military was in no position to defend the territorial integrity of the state or the lives and property of the people. Its 3,500–4,000 personnel were ill-prepared; its logistical support and levels of arms and ammunition totally inadequate.

By 1996, when a democratically elected civilian government was installed, it was apparent that there was an urgent need to reform the Ministry of Defence (MoD) and the military in general. Sierra Leone needed well-trained, effective and disciplined armed forces and a transparent, accountable military structure subject to democratic civil control. In essence, this was why the Sierra Leone Security Sector Programme (SILSEP) began work to restructure the MoD and restructure and retrain the RSLAF.

MoD restructuring saw the transformation of a state department that had hitherto been a 'clearing-house' for all military financial matters to an institution which ensured democratic oversight and accountability of the armed forces. This restructuring process involved a wide range of issues, from the formulation and implementation of a strategic defence policy to making the RSLAF broadly representative, non-partisan, professional and democratically accountable.

The success of the reforms in both the MoD and the RSLAF depended on:

- A clearly defined objective, particularly in an environment where the majority of military personnel lack insight as to why they and their institution need to be transformed
- Allaying fears and apprehension of the people about how reforms would affect them, either directly or indirectly
- Matching social realities of mass unemployment with political exigency

Thus there was a need to inform both RSLAF personnel and the people of Sierra Leone of all steps taken to restructure the MoD/RSLAF. This was tacitly explained by the president when he stated in the foreword of the white paper that 'with openness, responsiveness and accountability forming the cornerstone of Government policy this White Paper… explains how our thinking is being shaped and influenced by internal and external threats… The key to this rests in having an effective and affordable defence policy that can sustain the long- term peace and security needed.'

Purpose of the Defence White Paper

As reforms of Sierra Leone's defence system progressed, the MoD embarked on writing the defence white paper. Its aim was to explain to the people what steps had been taken thus far to restructure the MoD and RSLAF, and initiate a wider consultative process that could take their views into account when designing a strategic defence review of the armed forces. The overall objective of the paper was to create an environment where the RSLAF would be able to operate under the guidance of a comprehensive and codified defence policy.

Unlike many defence white papers, the Sierra Leone paper deliberately goes beyond the consultative process. It explains not only the substantial progress made, but also outlines past and present shortcomings and the MoD's aspirations for the future. This wider scope was intended to provide the people of the country with sufficient information to allow them to form opinions on defence in general, as well as on military personnel and their welfare and the new management of MoD/RSLAF structures. The paper was also designed to serve as the stream from which the people could source information to help them make informed judgements about how best to allocate government funds for defence purposes. The defence white paper is the first time in the history of Sierra Leone that a document was published whose main objective was the right of the people to know and be informed.

The Defence White Paper Process

The process of compiling the paper involved a wide range of consultations within and outside the country's defence system. Stakeholders were consulted on their respective roles and their interface with defence-related institutions throughout the government's restructuring exercise and beyond. However, apart from the Campaign for Good Governance (a Sierra Leonean non-governmental organisation supported by the National Democratic Institute), consultations involved government ministries, departments and agencies that have direct dealings with the MoD and the military. In addition, members of parliamentary subcommittees on defence and finance were consulted. This process enabled an in-depth informative document to be prepared on work performed to date and future plans and strategies for the RSLAF.

The approach used in the development of the paper was consultative and participatory. It was designed to ensure that all those involved in the restructuring process were able to understand their roles and responsibilities within the larger goal of making the RSLAF a democratically accountable force. At the same time, the process sought the support of the political head of the MoD, particularly in the area of the future role of the military.

At the MoD level, a proposal for the paper was put forward to the Defence Policy and Operations Committee (the highest policy-making body) seeking approval for a separate committee to manage the paper's information-gathering process. The proposal was discussed thoroughly; approval was given for a committee of representatives from the Ministries of Foreign Affairs and Internal Affairs, Sierra Leone Police (SLP), Office of National Security (ONS), Marine Resources and a civil adviser, among others. After a number of consultations, a template of what to include in the paper was designed and agreed upon, although there were slight differences of opinions as to whether the white paper should precede a defence review or wait until a national security policy had been designed. Because the ONS was only at its teething stage in the early 2000s, a number of stakeholders felt there was a fundamental need to inform the people on developments undertaken to date in restructuring the military. The director of defence policy persuaded the Defence Policy and Operations Committee of the importance of taking work on the paper forward. This, the director of defence policy argued, would lay the foundation for a future defence review that would be inclusive and embrace divergent opinions throughout the country.

On the basis of the template, a consultative tour was organised to visit all RSLAF brigade headquarters and some strategic battalions to gather accurate, first-hand information from troops on their perception of the restructuring exercise and other issues affecting their welfare. The team also wanted to assess current deployment strategy and determine the present state of national security and future operational needs. The consultations supported the development of informed recommendations regarding the paper that could be used to convince the government of Sierra Leone and the donor community of the need to provide more resources for the restructuring and democratisation of the RSLAF.

While consultation within the RSLAF was under way, the team also embarked on a series of meetings with civil society organisations on the issue of military restructuring and their vision for the RSLAF. These meetings were very fruitful; for one thing, civil society saw the process as a novelty, as it was the first time the people had been consulted about government policy in such a comprehensive fashion. Of particular note was the emergence of strong public opinion about poor troop living conditions. For example, in the towns of Kono and Kabala the people, including area parliamentarians, not only strongly advocated improved living conditions, but asked for a review of the design and structure of Operation Pebu. They requested a government/international effort to improve troop living conditions that had been widely criticised. Furthermore, they expressed dismay over the poor state of logistics and communication within RSLAF operational areas. With those concerns, it became glaringly clear that the defence white paper should focus on troop conditions and welfare, as well as on the overarching goal of the military performing its constitutionally mandated duties.

At the completion of the consultative exercise, harmonisation of the findings was completed and a report was submitted to the MoD. However, the report was not well received by the joint support commander of the UK International Military Assistance Training Team (IMATT). Criticism of the report included accusations that it was 'imaginary' and geared towards 'discrediting' the efforts of the military high command. Notwithstanding such condemnation, the Defence Policy and Operations Committee gave clearance and support for the drafting of the first defence white paper. This was completed and circulated to members of the committee itself and the SILSEP team in the UK for their professional comments and input. Their comments, in turn, were incorporated where appropriate into the draft of the paper; a number of meetings were held to discuss further issues raised in the document. A second draft was produced and submitted to the committee, where approval was sought for its submission to the Defence Council for publication approval. Upon submission to the Defence Council, the contents were thoroughly discussed and approval given for publication of the white paper for public consumption. It should be noted here that because of inexperience in writing such a defence policy document and the relative newness of members of the committee to democratic management of defence, contributions from committee members were not so much concerned with substantive content, but more with language and style.

Contributions from the UK SILSEP team were tremendously helpful in terms of contents, style and presentation of the final paper. However, as discussed below, tension arose between Freetown and London on the nature and scope of the paper.

To indicate the importance of the people in the process of democratising the military, the president launched the white paper in the presence of all paramount chiefs and other traditional leaders in the country, and stressed the importance of their contribution in designing the size and shape of the armed forces. Publication of the defence white paper provided the basis for future discussion of structural reorganisation and management of the RSLAF, and helped focus on rightsizing of the military to make it robust and operationally effective. The RSLAF is now closer than it ever was to being equipped with the skills, knowledge and sense of discipline required to perform its duties.

Output of the Defence White Paper

Stemming from the defence white paper, a fundamental reorganisation of the RSLAF and MoD ensued, with special attention paid to restructuring and streamlining the armed forces. This involved the creation of a new military structure within and outside the MoD by:

- Merging the joint support and joint force commands into a single RSLAF command structure
- Establishing a new assistant chief of defence staff at the MoD in charge of personnel and training
- Ensuring that the director of organisation management and audit reports directly to the deputy minister of defence instead of to the director general, who serves as the MoD's vote controller

This process also involved reorganisation of committee structures within the MoD to ensure efficient MoD/RSLAF management. This reorganisation was made with particular emphasis on financial management that guarantees transparency, accountability and probity. In adhering to the government policy of rationalising the defence budget, the armed forces were to be downsized to create savings, which could then be reinvested back into the RSLAF to make it leaner and more robust in the longer term.

The most important result emanating from the defence white paper was improved clarity of roles within the RSLAF, between the MoD and the joint force command and the sometimes difficult relationship between civilians and military staff working at the MoD. In 2003 the Command Structure Review Committee began to review the structure of the MoD/RSLAF established by the MoD advisory team and IMATT. The committee's objective was to adapt the structure designed by the UK government to local needs and culture and ensure that local participation and ownership were incorporated in any new structural design that emerged from the command structure review. Thus membership of the Command Structure Review Committee was purely Sierra Leonean, with IMATT and the MoD's civil adviser providing technical advice on how the exercise should be conducted. At the end of the exercise, a structure emerged that reflected the aspirations of a majority of Sierra Leonean players in the area of management and governance of the country's defence system. It was endorsed by both the Defence Policy and Operations Committee, chaired by the deputy minister of defence, and the Defence Council, headed by the president.

The Role of Advisers in the Defence White Paper Process

In keeping with the concept of local ownership of the reform process, MoD advisers, particularly the civil adviser and related personnel at the UK MoD, embarked on a policy of enhancing the capacity of Sierra Leonean civil servants through mentoring. In particular, the director of defence policy was focused on policy design and analysis, while the deputy minister and other MoD senior staff were encouraged to cooperate, support and participate in the process of collating information for the defence white paper. Meanwhile, the UK Department for International Development (DFID) provided opportunities for overseas study tours for comparative country case studies in South Africa and the UK. The most fundamental role of external advisers in the writing of the defence white paper was that of editing the final version for publication. This role was appropriate, as it allowed an incisive review of the issues and a comparison of past, present and future responsibilities and management of the RSLAF before the document was launched by the president.

Local Ownership

From the outset, the director of defence policy was determined to ensure that work on the defence white paper was steered by Sierra Leoneans, while recognising the important role of UK advisers, who were always ready to help.

Notwithstanding this determination, the director was faced with the challenge of convincing external advisers of the importance of Sierra Leonean context, both in terms of the paper's content and, perhaps more importantly, in the process of developing and publishing the paper. For example, during development of the paper some advisers observed that 'the Paper appeared to us to contain the kind of detail and direction that we would expect to see in a completed White Paper, written after a Defence Review and full country-wide consultation'. What they did not understand at the time was that the people of Sierra Leone had not been involved in or informed about the military reform process. Therefore, any attempt to undertake a defence review would mean, in the first instance, informing them of developments undertaken so far in order to enable them to contribute to such a review from an informed point of view. Thus the defence white paper would perform the function of preparing the public for the scheduled defence review.

In another instance, while the UK civil adviser to the MoD supported the idea of continuing work on the paper, the IMATT commander wanted a defence review to precede it – a disagreement that created a rift between the two personalities involved. These differences aside, the civil adviser continued his support for the writing of the paper, as it was what the Sierra Leoneans wanted at that point in time. That support strengthened the determination of the director of defence policy to continue work on document. Meanwhile, it was apparent that the only thing advisers based in UK could do was support to the process by asking the civil adviser to work closely with the director of defence policy to complete the piece. The civil adviser was requested to edit the draft paper, remove some of the details and change some of the statements relating to the RSLAF's future direction. It should be noted that all work performed by the adviser was in full consultation with the director of defence policy and approved by the Defence Policy and Operations Committee; also, the character and determination of the director of defence policy guaranteed local ownership of the process. Without the director's commitment to local ownership, the whole process might have been hijacked or micro-managed by foreign advisers.

Challenges

Notwithstanding the successful production of the defence white paper narrated above, the process was faced with a number of challenges. Among these were engaging the interest of both civilian and military personnel in the process. Most MoD/RSLAF personnel were disinterested, because they felt the exercise was tedious and had no immediate tangible gains.

There was also the challenge of securing adequate funding to organise and undertake nationwide consultations. Generally speaking, the defence funding situation seriously affected the implementation of some of the issues contained in the paper. For example, in 2004 the MoD bid for Le58.8 billion to run its business and the Ministry of Finance announced an allocation of Le42.7 billion, thus leaving the MoD with a shortfall of Le16.1 billion. Significantly, while an amount of money was thus allocated, the MoD remained unable to access these funds. This situation left the MoD with the problems of payments to personnel retired under the restructuring exercise, subsidies to those wounded in action (WIA) and to families of those killed in action (KIA) and funding of adequate troop living accommodation and mobility and communications equipment.

All these issues had a telling effect on the force training cycle, command and control and rapid response capability of the RSLAF. It was this state of affairs, coupled with the planned draw-down of the UN Mission in Sierra Leone (UNAMSIL), which led DFID to give direct budgetary support to the MoD to effect payment to officers retrenched under the rightsizing programme and to WIA and KIA beneficiaries.

There was also a challenge in ensuring that IMATT officers relinquished executive roles and reverted to their initial advisory functions. The snag here was that there was a dearth of competent officers grounded in the modern concept of democratic governance of the military. This is what I call the 'donor's dilemma', because it became apparent that either the MoD/RSLAF achievements would become stunted by allowing Sierra Leoneans complete control of MoD affairs, even when it was clear that they were still grappling with the new concept of defence reform in post-conflict countries; or IMATT would continue to perform some executive roles to ensure sustained professional transformation of the MoD/RSLAF, thereby undermining the concept of local ownership.

This was not an easy challenge to overcome, but a minimalist approach that returned IMATT to its advisory role was eventually employed. In addition, there was the difficult situation faced by MoD civilian employees when IMATT officers refused to accept input from them on topical issues, insinuating that civilian ministry employees lacked the competence to make informed contributions. This issue created a great deal of tension between MoD civilians and IMATT officers. For example, when the civilian/military team (including representatives of IMATT) submitted their report on the brigade and battalion HQ tour, the IMATT joint support commander debunked the report's contents, claiming that it did not reflect the on-the-ground reality observed during the tour. There were instances when intimidating tactics were employed to prevent officers from making objective contributions that could lead to outcomes unexpected or unwanted by IMATT.

There was also the great challenge of ensuring UK agreement to open debate and transparency in decision-making and accounting practices, particularly with regard to the disbursement and management of UK funds. For example, when questions were asked on how decisions were arrived at for the procurement of over 100 used/reconditioned Land Rovers for the RSLAF, the response from IMATT was that it was UK money and that UK decisions were not accountable to the MoD. In other instances, military officers who challenged the views or positions of IMATT officers were seen as negatively impacting the SSR process and potentially dangerous to the new army, and were subsequently ostracised. Added to this was the issue of IMATT commanders gaining direct access to the president by bypassing the MoD chain of command, a situation that undermined the MoD's authority.

Above all was the challenge of ensuring that members of the RSLAF accepted the principle of civilian oversight. Due to the culture which had dominated the armed forces until then, many members of the RSLAF perceived that civilians had taken their jobs from them and a signal was being sent that the RSLAF was not competent. To some extent, this issue still exists today; it exacerbates latent tensions in the MoD and affects the civil-military defence management partnership.

For instance, the military continues to see civilian defence employees as inexperienced in defence and security issues and therefore lacking in competence to manage and oversee them. On the other hand, civilians see most of the higher echelon of the military as obstructing the reform process. This mutual distrust undermines MoD management to the degree that, for example, there is no commitment by the senior military cadre to participate in Procurement Committee meetings. This situation makes it difficult, if not impossible, to collect accurate information. The (partially true) argument of the military is that since the director general has tended to have a set position before meetings, it would have been meaningless for military officers to contribute. At the same time, there is the perennial problem of senior military programme managers dodging assignments, due to either incompetence or negligence, which forces the director general to ask his civilian directors to undertake jobs that should have been done by the military. The bottom line of this mistrust between civilians and the military has to do with who 'controls the purse' and, in a larger sense, with the reality that changing an organisational culture takes a considerable amount of time.

Conclusion

The publication of the defence white paper in Sierra Leone was a watershed in the history of governance and management of defence in the country. It laid the foundation upon which all reform programmes, including the future size and shape of the armed forces, have been built. The paper contained lucid guidelines as to the direction of the country's defence reforms *vis-à-vis* where the defence system had been prior to the restructuring process. However, the process involved in writing the paper indicated that MoD/RSLAF restructuring should not be focused only on force reduction and strengthening institutional capacity. It should also take into account the provision of adequate financial resources that guarantee the institution's capability to deliver its assigned tasks. At the same time, the perennial problem of accessing allocated financial resources has made it difficult for the MoD to implement fully its desire to reform the RSLAF into a lean, affordable and capable force for Sierra Leone.

The strong commitment of the government of Sierra Leone to SSR and the support of the UK government played a crucial role in seeing the defence white paper published. In addition, the role of civil society organisations in the process indicated the importance of their involvement in the reform of the military. Finally, a conclusion that emerged out of the defence white paper process is that external advisers should never display a 'know-it-all' or 'do-it-for-them' attitude. If the principle of local ownership is to take root, a 'do-it-with-them' attitude on the part of advisers is the most effective method to engender sustained development achievements in a post-conflict country such as Sierra Leone.

Chapter 10

Reforming and Building Capacity of the Sierra Leone Police, 1999–2007

Kadi Fakondo

Introduction

By 1999 it became obvious by every standard that the Sierra Leone Police (SLP) needed immediate reforming in order to regain both public confidence and international credibility. At the time the SLP was considered a spent force, with little or no logistical support to enhance its capability. Its methods of policing were very unprofessional and displayed blatant disregard for human rights; corruption was the order of the day. Morale and motivation among police personnel were very low.

This was the state of affairs when the incumbent President Ahmad Tejan Kabbah appointed Keith Biddle, a retired UK police officer, as inspector-general of police (IGP) in November 1999. At the time of his appointment, Biddle was head of the Commonwealth Police Development Task Force, which was transformed into the Commonwealth Community Safety and Security Project (CCSSP) in 2000. The main focus of the CCSSP was to support SLP operational activities, including capacity-building, in order to enhance prompt and effective response to crime and public disorder.

Under Biddle's leadership, comprehensive reforms of the SLP occurred, leading to a much more transparent and accountable police force increasingly responsive to the needs of the people. It is important that we look at the details of the reforms that took place in the SLP within the period under review.

Institutional Reform

Ranking system

One of Biddle's first restructuring moves was to flatten the ranking system in the SLP from 22 ranks to ten, in order to focus the force on its roles and responsibilities. This move ended past confusion about roles and responsibilities and also shortened the communication hierarchy.

The Executive Management Board

Before Biddle's appointment, the IGP office was so powerful that everything emanated from and ended there. There was no recognition of the value of teamwork in decision-making, let alone the freedom to use one's own initiative. Upon assuming office, Biddle appointed a team of officers from the senior cadre to assist him in managing the force. This body became known as the Executive Management Board, the highest decision-making body in the SLP. Members of the board were senior assistant commissioners who shared national-level responsibility for personnel, training and welfare, professional standards and support services. Regional commanders were also appointed to assist the IGP in the four regions of the country. Teamwork became the benchmark of Biddle's administration.

The Operational Support Division

The Operational Support Division (OSD) is the armed wing of the SLP. Its personnel were heavily involved in fighting alongside government troops during the war. After the war, their strength was too small to cope with rising security demands; restructuring was in order. Under Biddle's dynamic leadership, with strong support from the CCSSP, the OSD was restructured by another UK adviser, Ray England. The OSD was divided into several professional units capable of meeting the country's internal security needs.

- The Police Support Group is responsible for maintenance of public order, cordons, searches and raids, and renders assistance at major disasters and incidents.
- The Static Protection Group provides protection for key installations, institutions, premises and strategic locations.

- The Mobile Armed Response Group responds to armed attacks on key personalities, installations, institutions, premises and strategic locations.
- The Armed Intervention Group resolves armed sieges and hostage situations.
- The Close Protection Group provides bodyguards for key personnel, e.g. the president, vice-president, cabinet ministers, diplomats, visiting VIPs, judges and senior police officers.
- The Training Group is responsible for training all units mentioned above.

As a result of this robust restructuring process, conducted since 1999, the OSD can now meet international standards and the country's internal service delivery needs.

New SLP departments

The restructuring process also established new departments in order to respond adequately to the policing needs of the people. These departments include:

- Family Support Unit – FSU
- Major Incident Support Team – MIST
- Complaints, Discipline and Internal Investigation Department – CDIID
- Community Relations Department – CRD
- Media and Public Relations Unit – MPRU
- Corporate Services Department – CSD

Police divisions were restructured as local command units; their commanding officers, formerly referred to as chief police officers, became local unit commanders. Police stations and some barracks were constructed throughout the country to provide adequate office space and accommodations. The police training school at Hastings was refurbished and new structures were built to strengthen its training capability. Work is in progress to transform the school into a police academy, in order to provide a more professional curriculum and expand in-service training.

Capacity-Building

An integral component of the restructuring process was capacity-building in terms of manpower and resources. Various training programmes at both national and international levels were pursued to enhance skills development and professionalism. A good number of senior officers were sent to the UK to pursue an international commanders' course. Senior officers also benefited from senior management courses delivered by the Institute of Public Administration and Management at the University of Sierra Leone. Other courses at the national level, including basic Criminal Investigation Department (CID) and FSU courses, research methodology and management courses and development courses for sergeants and inspectors, are delivered periodically. The capacity of vehicles and communications equipment has been greatly improved. The SLP now has over 800 vehicles and communications coverage almost everywhere in the country.

The Family Support Unit – A Case Study of the SLP Restructuring Process

The FSU started as a domestic violence unit which I established at the Kissy police district headquarters in Freetown. After the January 1999 invasion of Freetown by the Revolutionary United Front, I was posted as commander of the Kissy Division, a district which was home to thousands of ex-combatants and their 'wives' and other relatives. As the so-called 'wives' struggled to regain their freedom (for jungle justice was no longer applicable in the city), there was stiff resistance on the part of the ex-combatants, who wanted to control them. This precipitated a dramatic rise in domestic violence cases, which overwhelmed my personnel; I decided to create a special unit to handle them.

When the CCSSP brought in expatriate CID trainers from Britain in 2000, IGP Biddle, Bill Roberts, a UK adviser, and I considered it appropriate that the domestic violence unit be developed into a more comprehensive unit to respond not only to sexual offences, but also cruelty against women and children. After deliberations between police headquarters and the CCSSP, the unit was transformed into the FSU and officially launched. It became a unit under the CID with a director at police headquarters answerable to the director of crime management. We launched a major FSU publicity campaign in all broadcast and print media and in schools, markets, youth groups and area organisations. As a result, the FSU became a household name and everybody became interested.

Massive training exercises were conducted by CDIID trainers to equip the police to investigate sexual offences, domestic violence and child abuse and to meet the increasing number of cases reported. We also established partnerships with other organisations interested in protecting women and children from abuse. For example, the International Rescue Committee (Rainbo Centre) provided (and still does) free medical examinations and treatment for all victims. The Ministry of Social Welfare provided social workers who were trained with FSU police officers in joint investigations of sexual abuse. (During joint investigations, the police look for criminal elements involved in prosecution, while the social workers look at issues of victim and child protection.)

The UN Children's Fund (UNICEF) provided motorbikes and other forms of assistance for FSUs, the CCSSP funded all the training and the FSU was ultimately established in 26 police divisions country-wide. UN Civilian Police Force (CIVPOL) officers also worked with the FSUs all over the country and were very impressed with their effectiveness and professionalism. With their assistance, UNAMSIL provided training for FSU personnel. Senior CIVPOL officers were attached at FSU headquarters to advise and mentor personnel working in the unit.

The Justice Sector Development Programme (JSDP) replaced the CCSSP in 2005 with a view to establishing safety, security and access to justice for the people of Sierra Leone, especially for the poor, vulnerable and marginalised. The JSDP used a multi-sector approach, working with government and civil society to deliver even-handed justice. This programme still addresses judicial issues such as prisons, police (especially the FSU), juvenile justice, human rights and gender issues.

In 2006 I was appointed chair of the JSDP task force, which comprised justice sector middle-management officials. We met often with the JSDP team to develop of a strategic plan for the justice sector that reflected the needs of sector institutions and civil society. The JSDP constructed FSU offices at police stations in, among other places, Lumley, Kissy, Cabala Town, Waterloo, Tombo and Goderich. (It had already built the pilot office at the Moyamba police station.) The programme also supplied FSU office furniture, including televisions and videos for abuse victims and children's toys for interview rooms. Plans are in place to construct seven additional FSU offices in the provinces.

Even though there was much delay in dealing with FSU cases in courts, we still achieved enough convictions to send a clear message to the public that sexual offences and cases involving protection of women and children from abuse are considered very serious matters. With the help of two British judges in the High Court, sentences of up to 16 years' imprisonment were handed down. Convictions were also achieved in the provinces, thereby increasing public confidence in the FSU and the courts. This led to a great increase in the number of cases reported. Today, Sierra Leoneans realise that no one will be spared in the dispensation of justice to vulnerable women and children.

International Recognition

In June 2005 UNICEF Liberia requested the SLP to train the Liberia National Police (LNP) in the investigation of sexual exploitation and abuse in order to counteract the increasing occurrence of sexual offences in that country. The SLP was contracted after careful observation of police institutions in West Africa in their handling of women and children suffering from various forms of abuse.

The IGP, Brima Acha Kamara, approved the SLP contract to help the LNP establish an FSU prototype. Together with Sergeant (now Inspector) Vandi, we spent two months doing research and preparing a training package of international standards for Liberia. UNICEF Liberia requested the heads of NGOs and sexual abuse specialists from the UN Mission in Liberia to read and critique our training manual. In August 2005 we left for Liberia; training began with a colourful launch ceremony in full view of the mass media. A total of 25 male and female police officers were trained for one month; the headquarters of the Women and Children Protection Section, Liberia's FSU prototype, was established at LNP headquarters.

After multiple sessions, a total of 75 LNP personnel are now trained in family support issues and practices. We have also established units and deployed personnel in Monrovia and its immediate environs. Each of our training partnerships included mentoring and recommendations for further programme improvement. In late 2006 we returned to Liberia to carry out training of trainers, and subsequently returned to observe roll-out of training led by Liberian nationals.

Both the UN and Liberians were satisfied with the operation of the Women and Children Protection Section. While, as in Sierra Leone, conviction rates in court rose, though were not very satisfactory, the process of protecting victims has expanded from Sierra Leone to Liberia – a remarkable partnership in the name of individual security.

Impact of the Restructuring Process on the Sierra Leone Police

There is no doubt that the SLP restructuring process has both positive and negative ramifications.

Positive impacts

The SLP restructuring process has greatly increased the service delivery capacity of the police. With improved logistical supply, the force has been able to reduce crime rates around the country. Experience has shown that violent crimes are rampant in post-conflict countries, but we have managed to be on top of our situation. (It is important to recognise that crime can never be totally eradicated.)

As a result of rapid training (recruitment) exercises, the strength of the force has risen to about 9,500 personnel. This has greatly increased police visibility in our communities. The restructuring process also exposed a good number of SLP personnel to national and international training. Over 150 senior officers have attended the UK international commanders' course. Junior officers have attended training sessions in Ghana, Nigeria, India, Botswana, South Africa and other countries. This has enabled the force to meet international standards and led to the aforementioned training partnership with Liberia. Since then, SLP officers have served in UN peacekeeping missions in Haiti; currently, they are serving in Sudan's Darfur region.

SLP bureaucratic and regimental bottlenecks in the past were perhaps the greatest impediment to the force's progress. The reduction in the number of ranks from 22 to ten is viewed by many as the solution to this problem. Through command streamlining and an improved communications system, policies and communications from the IGP's office can now reach down the system to local constables anywhere in the country in a short period of time.

In the restructuring process a good deal of infrastructure development took place in the SLP. New police stations, posts and barracks were constructed all over the country. These improvements in working and living environments contribute to improved force morale and motivation. The restructuring process also brought new uniforms, which made us look smart. The public admire us and call us 'our police officers' with pride and dignity.

Establishment of the CDIID has resulted in personal accountability of every police officer. This system of checks and balances has helped reduce unprofessional and arbitrary behaviour and has increased public confidence in the SLP tremendously.

The introduction of community policing has bridged the gap between the police and the people. Local policing partnership boards were established in every division to enable community members to have a say in the policing of their neighbourhoods. Regular meetings are held with civilians to encourage them to assist us in day-to-day policing – we could never succeed without them.

Among the most important impacts of the SLP restructuring process is the improved respect for human rights. Before restructuring, people were kept behind bars for as long as the police wanted for very minor offences, such as common assault. There were blatant violations of human rights; cells were filthy and unfit for human habitation. In response to this violation of basic rights, human rights desks were created in police stations. Today we have police officers who routinely inspect stations for over-detention and cell conditions. UN Observer Mission (UNIOSIL) personnel also visit police stations to check the cells and interview inmates. I am proud to say that even juvenile detention is now a thing of the past in the SLP. However, despite our progress, the SLP is not perfect.

Negative impacts

The reduction of ranks in the SLP has become a major source of disgruntlement among affected personnel. During restructuring, the ranks of sub-inspector and corporal were taken away, without promoting those who held these ranks to inspectors and sergeants respectively. Instead, these ranks were demoted to sergeants and constables respectively, and were understandably demoralised and unmotivated. However, in the period before the 2007 elections these overlooked employees were promoted and the situation was redressed.

The high numbers of university graduates and other certificate holders in the SLP have created problems. Upward mobility for those who do not have certificates is now remote. Even graduates will find it difficult to move up the hierarchy, given that there are now only ten ranks.

Despite all the mechanisms put in place to make us professional, five police officers were dismissed last year for stealing exhibits. Another two were dismissed for raping a suspect in custody and charged in court. In late 2007 two police officers caught stealing National Power Authority fuel were dismissed and taken to court. This is a clear manifestation that there is no perfection anywhere; we are trying very hard to eradicate the unwanted elements.

Conclusion

From the above analysis we can safely conclude that it was extremely necessary to reform the Sierra Leone Police from what it was before 1999 to what it is today. We can now proudly walk along the streets of Sierra Leone and other countries as members of the Sierra Leone Police – *a force for good* – with a vibrant FSU protecting our women and children.

Chapter 11

Security Sector Reform in Sierra Leone and the Role of the Office of National Security

Kellie Hassan Conteh

Introduction

Sierra Leoneans are anxious to make individual and collective efforts to improve their country and its institutions, as we try to put behind us the most recent, ugly episode of conflict which ended in 2002. To that end, it is important to leverage lessons learned and past experience from Sierra Leone's security sector reform (SSR) process, and how we can share these lessons and good practices with the rest of the world.

In my mind, there are three significant reasons why Sierra Leone is an important case study for the international community. Firstly, the keen interest of the international community in developments in Sierra Leone underscores the phenomenon of why a collective global security action is required to resolve armed conflicts. Secondly, the international community may learn some positive lessons from the experiences in Sierra Leone that can be shared with other troubled areas in the global village. Thirdly, it is time to take stock and examine Sierra Leone's SSR process, a 'report card', so that we can further improve on how we should provide national security services based on democratic principles.

This chapter will address several issues:

- The significance of SSR in Sierra Leone
- The importance of the 2005 security sector review, including its production, key findings and recommendations
- The security sector reform implementation plan, November 2005–2010

- The 2002 National Security and Central Intelligence Act, which established the Office of National Security (ONS). Emphasis here is on the Act's provisions for coordination and oversight mechanisms within the security sector that have facilitated transparent decision-making at the highest levels
- The coordination of security provision during the 2007 general elections

The Significance of SSR in Sierra Leone

By the end of the Sierra Leone conflict in 2002, Sierra Leoneans had concluded that there must be a better way of defining and providing security for themselves and their country. They were no longer satisfied with the restrictive, conventional definition of security as military security; they had been exposed to this restrictive definition since colonial days. They realised that they deserve to live their lives with some degree of security from physical harm.

The experiences of the people of Sierra Leone during the war did not leave them with a good opinion of the delivery of physical security services by the existing security infrastructure. They had experienced the haphazard and uncoordinated way the war was conducted, resting on the pedestal of grotesque and uncorroborated intelligence support, which occasioned some of the greatest sufferings ever inflicted by man on fellow man.

For better or worse, the war acted as a catalyst to move the focus of security away from exclusive emphasis on uniformed security forces (military and police) towards personal security for individuals.

Thus it was no surprise when the democratically elected government, after returning from exile in 1998,[1] decided that a functioning security sector is a critical precondition for development. The government of Sierra Leone (GoSL) embarked on a programme to establish a coordinated security and intelligence architecture with oversight mechanisms. The focus and key principle were: without security, there could be no sustainable development.

To carry out the required restructuring of the sector, a security sector review was conducted, led by the ONS. The Sierra Leone Police (SLP) and the Republic of Sierra Leone Armed Forces (RSLAF) embarked on role-specific restructuring, which continues to this date. The ONS continues to grow and become more efficient in coordinating security sector activities. Since 2003 the sector has undertaken joint training activities embodied in study days and annual national security exercises.

During these exercises, Sierra Leoneans have practised individual and collective responsibility to respond to issues dealing with national security emergencies. These exercises have helped build much-needed trust and mutual respect among the various security sector institutions and actors. Perhaps more importantly, they have helped to build an understanding of our individual strengths and weaknesses and how we might all work together to achieve national security goals. This process gives the ONS the motivation and inspiration to lead in the formation of a national security policy, fine-tune procedures and establish mechanisms that foster cooperation and collaboration and strengthen oversight.

These initiatives have led to the development of policies covering a wide range of issues which had not been addressed before.

- Provision for military support to the civil authority, as detailed in the Sierra Leone military aid to the civil power (MACP) policy
- A protective security manual for government ministries and departments, which provides guidelines on how we can protect our key national assets. These guidelines range from public utilities to sensitive information relating to the country's defence and economy
- The Sierra Leone disaster management policy
- A standard operating manual for private security companies to help regulate the mushrooming private security industry
- Standard response guidelines to serve as a 'bible' for all security sector institutions on the *modus operandi* for dealing with national emergencies and the national security decision-making process

Apart from these key policy-making innovations, there have been several periodic security assessments to address emerging problems in need of GoSL attention. These assessments have greatly enhanced the decision-making process in post-war matters of national security.

The UK Department for International Development (DFID), supported by a defence advisory team well versed in multi-sector development, provided initial in-country advice to help give strategic direction to SSR. Subsequently it had continued to provide remote advice to the ONS. Equally, input by the International Military Assistance Training Team (IMATT) proved critical, as one of the serving UK officers at the time had the skill-set necessary to plan and carry out a security sector review. While it was a considerable setback to the process when he left, new Sierra Leonean staff were able to fill the gap.

To assist the national security coordinator, a secretariat was formed using ONS staff to provide both organisational and administrative support for the production of the security sector review.

The 2005 Security Sector Review

The security sector review process, begun in 2003, was vital in assessing the security requirements for a safe and enabling environment within a five- to ten-year period. The objective of the review was to evaluate the main threats to the political, social and economic development of Sierra Leone, identify relevant institutions to counter these perceived threats and develop appropriate and affordable strategies to address them.

Good practice dictated that to take SSR forward, a broad range of security sector stakeholders must be engaged. In Sierra Leone this range of stakeholders came to be known as the working group (WG). The WG comprised representatives from the military and police, prisons, fire service, civil society (including local and international NGOs and the media), members of Parliament, traditional rulers (paramount chiefs), youth and women's leaders, civil servants, the judiciary and the private sector. Difficulties arose when some institutions sent junior representatives to WG meetings, indicating that some decision-makers still saw security as an exclusively military issue. Later in the process, the ONS took on the role of ensuring that all parties understood why their input was of critical importance.

To initiate the work of the WG and give its members a focus for the security sector review, a framework document was prepared by the ONS. This assessment identified the threat areas of corruption, revenue loss, organised crime, subversion, cross-border issues, retardation, human rights violations by state actors and the confidence gap between the people and government.

The framework was endorsed by the National Security Council and work began in August 2003. While the list was (intentionally) not exhaustive, it helped shape subsequent discussions in WG committees. The WG also used the framework in a series of workshops held in all regions of the country to ensure critical buy-in outside Freetown.

The first step was to conduct a diagnostic assessment of the strategic vision for Sierra Leone. Participants were divided into syndicate groups to determine the kind of Sierra Leone they envisaged for the future, taking into account Vision 2025.[2] They were then tasked to identify threats that would jeopardise the attainment of Vision 2025. Wider public consultations were also held, for example through radio programmes.

The WG then conducted a series of workshops to produce a comprehensive security sector review that would include:

- A review of the existing security policy framework and an examination of existing institutions responsible for countering specific threats
- A review of the security architecture required to curb threats and identify where effective coordination was required between institutions and how such coordination could be delivered most effectively
- Establishment of an individual institutions/agencies policy framework to identify the role that security institutions must play to counter effectively threats that occur within their jurisdiction
- A gap analysis of the current role and capabilities of institutions and agencies against institutional requirements; on the basis of this analysis, a transformation strategy was developed

Implementation of the transformation strategy is an ongoing process; it continues to require the highest level of political commitment and support from all relevant stakeholders. In order to be successful, this strategy will also require the coordinated support, resources and expertise of donors.

Key Findings and Recommendations of the Security Sector Review

The security sector review was finalised and published in 2005. It identified external security threats to Sierra Leone as limited. Most of the identified threats come from within, including from the many ex-combatants across West Africa who are unemployed and impatient with the slow pace of development. Similarly, there are still thousands of small arms and light weapons in circulation in the subregion, which continue to be a threat to individual security.

The review identified the need for a smaller, more flexible RSLAF, but a larger SLP to deal with critical law enforcement problems. The principal work of these forces will need to be both intelligence-led and supported by a well-developed and better-equipped intelligence apparatus that ensures the appropriate focus of scarce resources and critical forewarning on threats to the stability of the state.

At the same time, relevant ministries and departments require considerable capacity-building programmes to minimise risks and vulnerabilities. These institutions should also complement the efforts of security services to ensure that instruments of other ministries, departments and agencies are deployed, including those in the diplomatic and economic spheres and civil society.

The following are key recommendations of the security sector review:

- Foster capacity-building of security sector institutions to ensure better alignment and performance and provide an enabling environment for development
- Institutionalise effective security partnerships, including the integration of efficient intelligence management mechanisms and non-state security actors
- Enhance security sector coordination and oversight mechanisms, redefine the composition of oversight structures and strengthen security sector parliamentary committees
- Increase the security architecture at the local level to help sustain the local governance decentralisation process

The 2002 National Security and Central Intelligence Act

Throughout the conflict, the country did not have a structured forum for intelligence coordination outside and independent of military structures. In other words, soldiers had no organised political direction. The public's experience of what this lack of coordination meant, coupled with an urgent desire to establish oversight mechanisms with civilian control of the security apparatus, led to the birth of the National Security and Central Intelligence Act in 2002.

The Act established the National Security Council, which is now the highest national security forum. It is chaired by the president; the vice-president is deputy chair. The council's membership includes the ministers of finance, foreign affairs, defence, internal affairs, information and broadcasting, and justice and the heads of the primary security institutions:

- The ONS, represented by the national security coordinator
- The SLP, represented by the inspector-general of police
- The RSLAF, represented by the chief of defence staff

These officials, who represent key security architecture institutions, provide technical support during deliberations. The NSC meets monthly.

A critical component of the Act was the establishment of the ONS itself, which serves as the secretariat for the NSC and coordinates security sector activities. In that position, the ONS translates policy direction from the NSC to doable missions and tasks for the security institutions to implement. It feeds assessments and recommendations from intelligence and security committees up to the highest political level and chairs the Joint Intelligence Committee (JIC) and the NSC Coordinating Group (NSCCG).

The JIC is a forum for the intelligence community to consider and endorse intelligence assessments provided by the ONS joint assessment team (JAT). The NSCCG includes the heads of security sector institutions and senior civil servants of relevant line ministries. It provides specific guidance in the implementation of NSC directives. The collaborative work of these bodies fosters cooperation and keeps individual security institutions fully aware of the overall direction of activities. Keeping in mind that none of these coordination mechanisms existed ten years ago, the fact that they were established is a major achievement. The Act also legalised the continued existence of the Central Intelligence and Security Unit (CISU), established by the government in the late 1990s. The CISU collects and assesses intelligence on activities that may constitute internal or external threats to the security of Sierra Leone.

The Act introduced for the first time an external dimension to Sierra Leone's intelligence efforts. However, while the legislation gave the ONS a welcome confidence boost, it did not resolve the critical issue of recruiting and retaining appropriate personnel. While it is much to the credit of the post-conflict government that functioning coordination of security was put in place, achieving political buy-in for the newly established ONS has proved to be a considerable challenge.

Periodic Security Assessments

Previously, intelligence and security services had simply written intelligence reports based on rumours and other unchecked sources. This ultimately led to not only an unreliable, but also a deeply politicised, intelligence service, whose reports targeted actual or perceived political opponents.

One of the significant results of the emerging structured approach to gathering and collating legitimate and vetted intelligence is periodic security assessments produced by the ONS. Intelligence reports and other forms of covert and overt reports are forwarded to the JAT in the ONS. These reports, based on national intelligence requirements, are collected by the intelligence agencies, recommended by the NSCCG and approved by the NSC as constituting the greatest threat areas for the state. Each intelligence agency works towards specific collection targets assigned and prioritised against given deadlines.

Upon receipt of the reports, the JAT assesses the issues as they impact the well-being of the state. These assessments are circulated to JIC members, who meet weekly to consider and may endorse, among other things, JAT assessments. Above all, these JIC deliberations are a built-in oversight mechanism ensuring that agencies limit their activities to national security issues. They also help avoid politically motivated intelligence analysis by 'situating the estimation' rather than 'estimating the situation', and vet assessments for veracity before they are forwarded to higher agencies and officials.

The critical process of identifying actions to be taken on the basis of intelligence reports is conducted within a forum that has wide ministerial and departmental participation, which ensures that a wide range of instruments at the disposal of the state are deployed. The ONS-led Strategic Situation Group comprises representatives from, *inter alia*, the Ministries of Defence, Foreign Affairs, Finance, Information and Internal Affairs. It is responsible for examining JIC-endorsed assessments in order to develop proposals for NSCCG action. In line with standard response guidelines, these proposals include recommendations on the most appropriate instruments of power to be deployed.

Coordinating Security for the 2007 General Elections

The August 2007 parliamentary and presidential elections were a litmus test for sounding the effectiveness of Sierra Leone's national security architecture and the coordinating role of the ONS. Under NSC leadership, security sector institutions were to stay neutral and impartial during the electoral processes. Thus during the elections politicians could not exploit divisions among the primary security forces and agencies; the security sector, coordinated by the ONS, spoke with one voice to the public and showed common resolve. This was done in a number of ways, in particular through statements from the sector broadcast on the radio.

The elections were a critical test for the security architecture of Sierra Leone, indeed for the country as a whole. There were two reasons for this.

They were the first post-conflict elections to be conducted using Sierra Leone's own resources and under the reformed post-war security architecture. Previous elections had been conducted under the umbrella of the UN Mission in Sierra Leone (UNAMSIL). They were also the first elections marking the end of a transition from one democratic government to another. The success of the electoral process was therefore an important pointer to building trust and confidence in the country's post-conflict transformation process, from a conflict state to a developmental state.

By mid-2006 the ONS JAT had begun to discuss the security needed to enable the conduct of free, fair and violence-free general and presidential elections. The assessment was a priority topic in the national intelligence requirements endorsed by the NSC.

These assessments identified potential areas of security concern in order to assist both the National Election Commission (NEC) and security sector institutions involved in election monitoring. Both the commission and targeted institutions then planned appropriate responses to threats to the election process. These potential threats included:

- Disruption and politicisation of party registration, constituency delimitation, voter registration, polling and campaigning, vote counting and the post-counting phase
- Specific problem areas such as the youth issue, arguments over party nominations, party court cases, ethnic, party and geographical affiliation, Freetown's cosmopolitan nature, the south-east issue and chiefdom boundary disputes

The NSCCG considered these assessments, identified specific actions to be taken and made recommendations for consideration by the NSC. It came to a point where the NSCCG often met several times weekly in the period preceding the elections. The following actions and recommendations were identified.

- Through a series of briefings, assure the diplomatic community of the government's determination to conduct a free and secure democratic process
- Explore possibilities for more financial and logistical assistance from the international community to ensure comprehensive support to areas which could affect the peaceful conduct of the elections

- Develop a GoSL information line to sensitise the public on the merits of citizens using non-violent means in seeking redress and expressing their political persuasions
- Encourage all, including civil society groups, community elders, traditional rulers and youth groups, to understand the need for security institutions to participate peacefully in the elections
- Encourage the NEC to work with the security sector and civil society to inform the public about election requirements and procedures
- Amend the MACP policy to empower the RSLAF to conduct border patrols without the SLP, which would need to muster all its manpower for internal policing during the elections
- Ensure that security sector activities are coordinated in collaboration with the NEC, so that scarce funds would be spent appropriately before, during and after the elections

The key judgement of this assessment was that the peaceful basis on which the elections were to be held was shaky and prone to erupt into violence unless overall efforts were well coordinated and focused. The methodology developed to address threat areas and help implement NSC-recommended actions was integrated into the NEC's concept of operation and collaboration with the security sector. As the elections approached, the threat assessment continued to be discussed and updated, in order to advise the government of the security climate.

The coordination forum provided by the ONS for the NEC, SLP and other security sector institutions engendered a structured approach that covered all phases of the election and resulted in successful security outcomes.

When the 2007 elections concluded, they were seen as a success for both security institutions and the comprehensive SSR process in Sierra Leone. However, rather than viewing this as a highlight, these security sector successes – and the exemplary leadership provided by the ONS – should be seen in the future as 'business as usual'.

Conclusion

The relatively violence-free 2007 elections were a genuine success for Sierra Leone – not only for the security sector but for the country as a whole. A new government was democratically elected and, importantly, the police and armed forces demonstrated a high level of professionalism during the electoral process. The SLP provided internal security; the RSLAF was only engaged through the MACP policy. By any measure, it is impressive that only five years after the end of conflict in 2002, the country's security sector was in a position to provide effective election security.

This, of course, does not mean that challenges to the ONS and other actors in the security sector have disappeared. There continue to be several issues that could threaten the stability of the security sector, and with it the stability of the country.

One of the key remaining concerns is the general financial weakness of Sierra Leone. Poor conditions of service in the civil service, for example, have led to low retention of trained staff, which leads to spending a disproportionate amount of scarce public funding on recruitment, induction and training, ultimately reducing effective service delivery. Under current financial circumstances, recruiting qualified individuals from the Sierra Leonean diaspora to strengthen civil service staff capability is impossible without significant subsidies from the donor community. Finally, it is worth remembering that conditions of service were one of the reasons why the armed forces revolted against the government in the early 1990s. At a very basic level, it was financial scarcity that led to the inability of the government to provide services to the population.

The quality of civil service staff is a challenge to the continued success and integrity of the ONS. Maintaining high-quality professional staff, backed by laid down codes of conduct at the ONS, has ensured that the institutions remain apolitical. As noted above, intelligence services in Sierra Leone during the 1980s and 1990s were used to subvert political opponents. The police and armed forces operated in silos; there was virtually no coordination of security activities. The fact that a rigorous process for intelligence gathering, collation and assessment is now in place and that Sierra Leone now has the ONS to coordinate security sector activities has proved that a fundamental overhaul of the security sector has occurred. However, these developments have taken place within a short period of time. Consolidating institution-building successes is a long-term process; we have much more work to do.

Notes

1 The democratically elected Sierra Leone government, run by the Sierra Leone People's Party, was exiled to Conakry, Guinea, in 1997 when the Armed Forces Revolutionary Council (AFRC) staged a coup. The government returned to power in 1998.

2 Vision 2025 provides Sierra Leone with a national vision for long-term development and projects future scenarios for political and economic progress. It gives a direction to Sierra Leone's medium- to long-term strategies, such as its poverty reduction strategy paper.

Chapter 12

Civil Society's Role in Sierra Leone's Security Sector Reform Process: Experiences from Conciliation Resources West Africa Programme

Rosalind Hanson-Alp

Introduction

In September 1990 a refugee walked into the Sierra Leone Police Special Branch, one of the country's intelligence-gathering services, and filed a 13-page report about an alleged plan to attack Sierra Leone. While the report was passed on through the security structures, there was no response in preparation for a potential attack.

Six months later, in March 1991, a Sierra Leonean soldier made a 17-page statement confirming the threat of an imminent border attack. As in 1990, the report passed through the security structures but there was no response.

Days later, attacks from the Liberian border in the east of Sierra Leone ensued, plunging the nation into more than ten years of a brutal war that claimed thousands of lives and devastated the country.

It is impossible to tell how events would have unfolded had the refugee's report been taken seriously by the authorities. What is certain is that security structures at the time were predominantly military-based and cooperation between civil society and the security sector was infrequent and tainted with distrust. Nonetheless, the fact that the second warning of an imminent border attack by a soldier was also disregarded indicates a more endemic, organisational failure by Sierra Leonean security forces at the time.

While the war officially ended in January 2002, Sierra Leone has been undergoing a security sector reform (SSR) process supported by the UK since 1999. It is internationally acknowledged that democratic oversight of the security sector contributes to good governance, accountability and transparency. Furthermore, in post-conflict societies such as Sierra Leone, effective and sustainable SSR is a crucial prerequisite for the consolidation of peace.[1] While the challenges of promoting practical civil society-security sector cooperation are many, the benefits of building such a relationship contribute to the prevention of internal as well as external threats to national security.

In the case of West Africa, the international community recognises the impact of ongoing SSR on most cross-border challenges and its potential to prevent relapse into regional conflict. In 2007 the UN Secretary-General's report on cross-border issues in West Africa[2] recognised the importance of SSR to conflict prevention and peacebuilding in the region, and highlighted the need to address cross-border issues more effectively. Crucially, the same report states that civil society has a vital role in SSR processes and that the establishment of sound civil-military relations is critical to good governance in the region. The report highlights the importance of linking civil society, social awareness and education in the fight against corruption in border areas by noting that 'when one witnesses soldiers with guns or police extorting money from motorists and market women, one cannot help thinking the battle against corruption is lost'.[3] The report also highlights how this type of petty corruption erodes state institutions and credibility, as populations give up all hope of changing the governance culture. This is of particular concern in Sierra Leone's Mano River Union subregion, where poor governance and corruption at local and district levels, simmering intra- and inter-community tensions, low-level conflict and cross-border security threats portend a relapse into widespread conflict.

The primary function of civil society is to provide oversight of security forces, including budgetary oversight, and to ensure their accountability and transparency. Civil society involvement is also likely to contribute to more effective and equitable decision-making and implementation, and provide the sector with a more comprehensive range of specialised, expert information. There is a role for civil society organisations in creating opportunities for dialogue among stakeholders, such as initiatives to build trust between communities and security sector forces.

It is also recognised that parliaments play a fundamental role in ensuring democratic oversight over the security sector.[4] Here, too, civil society organisations can play an important role in building parliamentarians' knowledge and skills about security. The experience in South Africa in the 1990s has shown that security and justice sector reforms are more effective and more sustainable if civil society supports the process and provides its expertise to parliaments and other oversight institutions.[5]

SSR in war-torn Sierra Leone presented two main challenges. Firstly, it was necessary to establish effective and accountable security agencies that could provide the security foundation for much-needed socio-economic reconstruction of the country and protect the state and its citizens. This had to be achieved against a history of politicised and unaccountable security sector forces and their fundamental breakdown during the war.

Secondly, it was necessary to establish effective civilian oversight of the restructured armed forces and security agencies. Historically, civil society had not actively engaged with the security sector in the country in any meaningful way.

Civil society's engagement with SSR in Sierra Leone has been slow and limited due to a combination of factors, including the scale of the task of reforming the sector in a post-conflict country, capacity issues and the need for a fundamental change in mentality. But it is happening and bridges are being built.

This chapter brings together experiences and lessons learned about the role of civil society in SSR in Sierra Leone as seen through the experience of the Conciliation Resources (CR) West Africa programme. CR started working in Sierra Leone in 1995 to support capacity-building efforts of civil society organisations to address the many challenges they faced in reducing the negative impacts of conflict on communities and promote reconciliation and peacebuilding. Over the years CR has responded to critical peace and security needs, largely focused in Sierra Leone, although some projects have a subregional focus. Our work has evolved under the thematic areas of community peacebuilding, subregional security and stability, and social exclusion and marginalisation, with a focus on women and youth.

CR's involvement in SSR in Sierra Leone has evolved from responding indirectly to the impact of reform on our peacebuilding work to a decision to engage directly with and contribute to the process. By working in partnerships, CR has engaged broadly with various aspects of the SSR process over the years, and more specifically with the impact of SSR on the communities and organisations with which it worked. For example, CR supported the work of civil society organisations in promoting the demobilisation and reintegration of Revolutionary United Front (RUF) combatants. It was part of two key civil society networks that analysed security issues and provided important entry points for the security sector to engage with civil society: Christian Aid's Partners in Conflict Transformation initiative and the Network for Collaborative Peacebuilding, now the West Africa Network for Peace – Sierra Leone.

Over time it became clear that responding only to the impact that SSR was having on our work was not the most useful way to engage with the process of peace consolidation in Sierra Leone. Through our work with young people, for example, we became aware of the tensions and mutual mistrust between youth and the security sector and the need to facilitate dialogue and promote information-sharing between these groups. CR started to directly engage in the SSR process through the *Strengthening Citizen's Security* pilot project. In 2007, CR formed a partnership alliance with the Mano River Women's Peace Network, the Centre for Development and Security Analysis and Search for Common Ground–Talking Drums Studio to pilot the Strengthening Citizens' Security project in Freetown, Kailahun and Kenema. This project was designed to reflect specific recommendations from the 2005 Sierra Leone Security Review[6] about the importance of and need for civilian involvement in the SSR process. As such, a guiding assumption of this project, funded by the UK Department for International Development (DFID), was that civilians have an active interest in participating in decision-making processes affecting their own security. The project, which ended this year, has helped facilitate dialogue and strengthen the relationship between the security sector and the civilian population.

CR's experience in Sierra Leone over more than a decade, through this project in particular, has provided useful insights on how the SSR process has approached engagement with civil society and civilians in general. The next section of this chapter provides a brief historic overview of the main characteristics of the security sector in Sierra Leone until the end of the war in 2002, and how it fundamentally shaped relations between the sector and civilians. The following sections look at implementation of the SSR process in the country *vis-à-vis* civil society engagement. The chapter then reflects on specific improvements and mechanisms for civilian oversight of the security sector that were established as part of the ongoing reform, informed by CR's experience with the Strengthening Citizens' Security project. The final section offers some concluding thoughts.

The Historic Relationship Between Sierra Leone Security Forces and Civil Society

The breakdown of trust between civilians and the security sector in Sierra Leone started well before the war. Three decades of single-party and military rule politicised the sector, eroded its professionalism and undermined civilian oversight.[7] Sierra Leone's security forces gradually became involved in politics: members of the military and police were intimately involved in government, including parliament, and either planned or supported three coups d'état. By the 1980s President Siaka Stevens had created his own loyal security force, the ruthless Special Security Division, which brought fear to the minds of many civilians and earned the nickname of 'Siaka Stevens' Dogs'. Political alliances with the army increased under the military rule of President Joseph Momoh, himself a major general, who succeeded Stevens in 1985. After 24 years of misrule, Sierra Leone was divided and economically and politically bankrupt; corruption was rife and the country was heavily dependent on foreign aid and loans. By 1992 the government's troops had not been paid for three months and frustration led to the ousting of President Momoh through a military coup. Young Captain Valentine Strasser emerged as the chairman of the National Provisional Ruling Council (NPRC) not long after the rebellion had begun, as the recently formed RUF crossed the border from Liberia in 1991.[8]

The NPRC promised to end the war and return the country to civilian rule, and announced the first multi-party elections since 1967. But after the initial high expectations for Strasser's 'Youth Revolution' and as the war continued to rage through the provinces, the NPRC regime was slow in implementing promises of change and soldiers regularly abused their power over civilians.[9] Despite having unique access to the RUF, it became increasingly clear to the general public that the NPRC lacked the capacity to take the peace process forward, and renewed offensives ensued with the RUF's takeover of Kono, Sierra Leone's principal mining district.

By 1995, as the long-promised election was nearing, a stalemate developed between a regime that had lost the population's trust and a rebel force that lacked widespread popular support. By then civilians were demonstrating an unequivocal desire to vote out the military. In fact, the brutality perpetrated against civilians by both government and rebel forces did not prevent civil society organisations from playing an active role in the national consultative conference of 1995, known as Bintumani I, with paramount chiefs, unions, academic institutions, journalists, the NPRC and other public institutions. This was an important opportunity for civil society representatives to express their views and play a part in the decision-making processes that led to the elections in 1996.

A week after a change in leadership of the NPRC in August 1996, the RUF declared a cease-fire under the condition that the election be postponed. This prompted a second round of consultations, known as Bintumani II, where civil society demanded overwhelmingly that elections take place on schedule. The government acquiesced and the Sierra Leone People's Party candidate, Ahmad Tejan Kabbah, became president.[10] However, civil society remained largely on the fringes of the Abidjan peace negotiations in 1996, which took place mostly outside Sierra Leone, thus preventing more meaningful local participation.[11]

In the first years following the end of the war in 2002, considerable focus was given to the restoration of the country's social fabric and infrastructure, both of which had been devastated during the conflict. The government directed its resources primarily to practical needs. Humanitarian aid, provided in large part by international non-governmental organisations (NGOs), flooded Sierra Leone in an attempt to address the breakdown of social structures and livelihoods and respond to the nation's psychological trauma.

Development agencies' efforts to foster community collaboration were often faced with public scepticism, making it difficult to create cohesion and encourage livelihood production. This widespread mistrust among Sierra Leoneans and their unwillingness to work as a community can be related to many factors. There was, of course, the trauma of the war and the brutality experienced by many civilians. In addition, people were forced to migrate to other areas and fend for themselves during the war, becoming more self-reliant, mistrusting others' motivations and believing there was more security in working independently. Some of the conflicts among communities and individuals that existed before the war were magnified by reprisals during the war. The conflict also reversed traditional social hierarchies when elders, who were traditionally protectors of the community, fled to safety while young people were encouraged to stay and defend the villages. At the end of the war, confidence in and respect for customary leaders among young people were significantly reduced; in some areas where they had been part of militias, the young were unwilling to relinquish power back to the returning traditional leaders.

In addition, Sierra Leone's history of military and, to some extent, police allegiance to politicians and authoritarian regimes had produced the widespread public view that there was no one to protect them. Rather than protect the population, the military committed the ultimate abuse of power when it turned against civilians and perpetrated appalling acts of violence and human rights abuses. This had a profound effect on people's opinion of security forces, particularly the military.

By the time the SSR process began in 1999, relations between civil society and the security sector were based on fear, suspicion and outright mistrust. Not surprisingly, the SSR process was met with immense public scepticism. While this was partly due to historic legacy, it was not helped by the initial lack of a clearly delineated reform strategy and poor communication with the public about the process.

Civil Society's Involvement in the SSR Process

As noted above, civil society has important oversight functions, promotes accountability and can contribute to decision-making processes through information sharing, training and building of security sector capacity. If in place, civil society, a critical element of democratic governance, helps avoid some of the historical problems Sierra Leone has experienced and can also help prevent a relapse into conflict. But to have a fully functional security sector with adequate civilian oversight, it is necessary to address the severe and crippling lack of resources and operational capacities of both government and civil society. In the Sierra Leonean post-conflict context, this has been one of the greatest challenges of the reform process.

By the time DFID's Sierra Leone Security Sector Reform Programme (SILSEP) was initiated in 1999, the concept of civil society involvement in SSR had not been formally outlined. In practice, civil society became involved on an *ad hoc* basis in the reform process as early as 1998, shortly after the restoration of the legitimately elected Kabbah government that had been overthrown in a coup in May 1997. As the government developed plans to create the new armed forces, it decided to include soldiers who had previously mutinied and joined the RUF. This controversial decision sparked a reaction by NGOs in October that year, leading to a meeting between 300 civil society representatives from all over Sierra Leone, the government and armed forces representatives. As a result, civil society proactively influenced SSR by making a range of proposals that promoted civilian involvement in the process, such as the circulation of pictures of all recruits so that ordinary Sierra Leoneans could vet them for previous human rights abuses.[12] While the government reacted positively to this engagement, implementation was hindered by the renewal of hostilities in 1999.

In 2000 collaboration between the Campaign for Good Governance,[13] the police, the Ministry of Defence and the Office of National Security (ONS) provided the opportunity for civil society to re-engage and respond to some of the controversial issues that were creating public concern. In particular, civil society was focused on highlighting a major public concern about the implications of reintegrating ex-combatants into the military and the future role of the Civil Defence Force,[14] which was, like the army, accused of committing human rights abuses during the war.

By mid-2001 a more formal policy emerged to ensure that SILSEP engaged with Parliament, civil society and the media. The UK, Sierra Leone's major international partner, made it clear that without establishing effective civil control over accountable and effective armed forces, long-term peace and stability would be difficult to achieve and sustain. This official recognition of fundamental tenets of civil society – transparency and accountability to the people – signalled that civil society could assist in the gathering of intelligence, report early-warning signs and participate in conflict resolution, thus contributing to SSR.

But despite these developments, for most Sierra Leoneans there was still very little knowledge or understanding of SSR as a structured process that involved strong collaboration between the UK and Sierra Leone governments, with input from the UN Mission in Sierra Leone (UNAMSIL). The government made little effort to communicate with the people about the few visible changes in the security sector that impacted on them directly, such as military and police reform. In fact, what little information was available to the people resulted in negative reactions.

For example, people were aware that SSR included absorbing ex-combatants in security forces. By 2002 approximately 2,300 ex-combatants from various factions had been absorbed into the new army through the military reintegration programme.[15] Combined with the public perception that the disarmament, demobilisation and reintegration (DDR) process rewarded the perpetrators of violence, this further deepened distrust of security forces in communities that had suffered brutality at the hands of these same soldiers. To make matters worse, in early 2003 a group of former soldiers and civilians attacked an armory in the outskirts of Freetown. A police investigation of the incident uncovered a plan by ex-combatants and soldiers to destabilise the country, allegedly to prevent the work of the special court set up to prosecute war criminals. These incidents only added to popular mistrust of an army tarred with a history of abuse and now composed of ex-combatants from different factions hiding under a national uniform.[16]

Despite these difficulties, the creation of the ONS in 2002[17] and the subsequent decision to carry out a review of the SSR process proved decisive in clarifying the approach to security specifically, and to its engagement with civil society and the people.

Making Security 'Everyone's Business'

Security na la man bizness is an expression in Krio[18] coined by security reformers in Sierra Leone. It means that security is everyone's business and is now widely used by both security sector personnel and civilians, which shows how much things have changed. Making security everyone's business became the explicit approach to SSR between 2002 and 2005, when a donor-driven change in paradigm and the Sierra Leonean government's commitment to it led to a change in focus from traditional state security to a people-centred view of human security.

But making security everyone's business was no minor task in a country like Sierra Leone, where the security/development nexus, or the lack of it, had contributed significantly to the cycle of poverty and conflict. Underlying the country's new approach was the belief that it was necessary to have a security sector that would not only help create an environment conducive to economic development, but also break the cycle of institutionalised violence. This required a fundamental change in mentality to replace unaccountable, politicised organisations that protected only the state's interests with a professional, transparent military sector capable of implementing the philosophy of human security.[19]

This new human security paradigm was embodied in the government's security sector review in 2005, which also linked the paradigm with the country's poverty reduction strategy, where security was identified as one of three pillars. The review explicitly recognised the value of civil society's involvement in security. President Kabbah stated this new paradigm in no uncertain terms to civil society, media and the public:

> SSR (Security Sector Reform) and the resulting improved security sector are there to serve you, the people. Security is no longer a secret; it is a public service, requiring public support and increased confidence... development needs security just as security needs development. Therefore, the successful implementation of the [security sector review] findings and recommendations outlined... must be a priority for all Sierra Leoneans.

While the government's security sector review offered a valuable critique, recommended institutional reforms and detailed specifically the institutions responsible for making them, it was not broadly communicated to the public. A large part of the population was unaware of the significant efforts to reform the sector and, most importantly, its implications for greater protection for citizens and civil society participation. In light of the legacy of a culture of silence, repression and mistrust, this would have been a good opportunity to dispel scepticism about the new security sector forces and the reform process. Nevertheless, visible steps have been taken to improve civilian oversight of Sierra Leone's security forces and promote engagement between them and civil society. Against a background of authoritarianism, bad governance and a devastating decade-long war, these important steps present opportunities that need to be seized by all relevant stakeholders.

Strengthening Human Security in Sierra Leone: Opportunities and Shortcomings

The current security architecture foresees improved civilian oversight mechanisms, including parliamentary oversight, and information sharing between civil society and the security sector that allows for a two-way flow of information from the grassroots to the presidential level. The architecture also calls for new, reformed military and police forces. The following analysis takes a closer look at what these proposed reforms offer in terms of civil society engagement and strengthened citizen security. It draws on CR and its partners' experience with the Strengthening Citizens' Security project to help better understand future opportunities and challenges.

Civilian Oversight of the Security Sector through Parliament

A fundamental element of civilian oversight of the security sector is to make it accountable to a democratically elected parliament. In the past, Sierra Leone Parliament's oversight functions, particularly under Siaka Stevens's one-party rule, were largely weak and ineffective, serving mainly to approve executive decisions. This left a legacy of unaccountability and lack of transparency, which the 2005 review addressed by recommending the transformation of coordinating and oversight mechanisms: 'reflecting on past evolutions in the security sector, civilian monitoring and oversight must be strengthened to ensure adequate transparency, accountability and responsiveness of the security forces'. The review went on to propose 'strengthening the Parliamentary Oversight Committee for the security sector… to ensure democratic governance of the sector'. This is no minor task.

The constitution of Sierra Leone provides legal authority for parliamentary oversight of government agencies, including ministries, the defence sector and security and intelligence agencies. The Parliamentary Oversight Committee on Defence, Internal and Presidential Affairs (POCDI&PA) is specifically responsible for oversight of the security sector, but it faces substantial challenges in performing this role effectively.

In April 2008, as part of the Strengthening Citizens' Security project, CR commissioned an assessment of the POCDI&PA.[20] The aim was to identify ways to build parliamentary oversight of the security sector, ascertain the policy, regulatory and material needs of the security-related parliamentary subcommittee and identify training needs for its members.

The majority of those interviewed for the assessment emphasised that there is a lack of clarity surrounding the committee's functions, noticeable in its name. While the committee's mandate is restricted to issues of defence, internal and presidential affairs and does not include security (police) and intelligence, it has effectively extended its remit to these areas. However, the police, Ministry of Defence and National Security Council still continue to approve national security policies. There is also an overlap between the committee's mandate and other parliamentary oversight bodies; the POCDI&PA does not have exclusive power and authority over defence appointments or budgetary issues.

As noted in the assessment:

> there was general concern about the existence of a plethora of oversight bodies provided for in the 1991 Constitution… and lack of clarity of the specific role of the Committee dealing with defence matters. Almost all those interviewed called for clarity of the functions of this Committee.

The assessment concludes that:

> the lack of clearly-defined legal authority to address complex defence and security issues such as procurement, budgeting and preparedness of military units for international cooperation adversely affects the political will to effectively promote democratic control and transparency on security matters.[21]

The assessment also highlighted other challenges, such as the committee's lack of human, financial and material resources. According to the assessment, selection of the 16 committee members, of whom only one is a woman, is not based on knowledge of the security sector; appointments occur through consultation with party leaders in Parliament. In the 2007 general elections, approximately 80 per cent of elected parliamentarians were new; many had returned home from living in the diaspora. The assessment noted that most committee members:

> still see security matters in terms of state security and the physical security. They do not see it in human security terms, which has implications for their role in broader security matters.

The assessment also noted that the committee's support staff do not have specialised knowledge of security matters.

NGOs such as 50/50 Women's Group, the Campaign for Good Governance and CR, as well as the ONS, have facilitated a series of workshops and training sessions to build Parliament's capacity on a number of issues, including SSR and oversight. But much more needs to be done to increase parliamentarian and POCDI&PA capacity to perform effective security sector oversight functions.

Civil Society Engagement through Provincial and District Security Committees

As mentioned above, opportunities for civil society involvement in the security architecture exist at the level of provincial and district security committees (PROSECs and DISECs), which were established to serve as early-warning mechanisms at the community level. PROSECs are security committees based in each provincial capital that provide early warning to the government of the existence or likelihood of any security threat to the province, the country or the government. They submit fortnightly reports to the Joint Intelligence Committee (JIC). DISECs are the equivalent security structure at the district level; they submit weekly reports through their respective PROSECs. The committees are composed of representatives from the ONS, provincial and district civil service, traditional security forces and civil society represented by traditional authorities from the Paramount Chiefs Committee. Temporary membership is given to civil society representatives when they are relevant to a particular security-related circumstance, such as the National Electoral Commission during national and local elections. Each committee offers limited membership to an additional civil society representative, who participates in non-classified portions of meetings on the premise that this can bring the voice of the people to the security table.

In principle, PROSECs and DISECs provide important mechanisms where civil society representatives meet with security personnel to assess local security issues, share and verify pertinent information and come up with a plan of action to address security threats. This gives civil society a voice in important security decision-making processes and provides a venue where the civil society and security sector relationship can be strengthened.

However, because of the legacy of public distrust and suspicion of the security sector, these committees are often perceived to be secretive and potentially opposed to civil society. Some security personnel have been reluctant to engage with civil society and NGOs, holding that security issues are 'secret' and not for public consumption. For example, one military officer challenged CR's involvement in security issues:

> What is Conciliation Resources doing with security? You NGOs should be engaged in relief and development issues, not in security. Security is the domain of institutions like the military or police, not NGOs. So what is your interest in this?

Another hurdle to overcome involves selection of civil society members, which has not always followed set criteria, but rather has relied on existing personal relationships between committee members and individual civil society representatives. Initially there were also difficulties with coordination and scheduling of meetings. However, ONS involvement in the process has since ensured that PROSECs and DISECs meet regularly and information filters through the system. As these groups began to work effectively, it became clear to both civil society and security personnel that once each party was able to express its concerns and misconceptions about the other, relationship-building between them led to good information sharing that benefited both citizens and the security sector.

The ONS has also begun to employ young professionals in district offices. Their enthusiasm and commitment to bringing security to the public forum has had a powerful impact on the civil society-security sector relationship. For example, in Kenema and Kailahun districts, following its participation in CR-facilitated meetings with civil society, the ONS has been eager to engage young people and other civil society representatives in security issues, such as collaborating on public campaigns against violence in elections (see Box 1 on page 202).

One of CR's partners, Search for Common Ground, has worked with community radio stations in Kenema and Kailahun districts to develop bi-weekly broadcasts focused on security. These 'Security Talk' programmes offer an opportunity for DISECs and local policing partnership boards (LPPBs)[22] to air information about their meetings.

Box 1. An entry point for civil society to engage in security processes through district security committees

Conciliation Resources facilitated open meetings between civil society and security sector personnel in Kailahun district, with the aim of improving local understanding of security structures and dialogue between security personnel and civil society.

During the first meeting, when security personnel presented the structure of national security, including the function and membership of Kenema's DISEC, it became evident that most civil society participants did not know that there was someone representing them in the DISEC. As one civil society participant stated, 'He does not represent us and we are not aware he sits on DISEC on our behalf.' At the same time, security personnel stated that this member was currently suspended from the DISEC during investigation of the allegation that he was a political aspirant, which, if true, would breach the criteria of political impartiality. The security personnel used this civil society representative to argue that civil society was neither serious nor committed to participating in security issues.

This issue highlighted some of the challenges of collaboration, and civil participants acknowledged that civil society was fragmented: 'there is no civil society here. I would like to ask that you [CR] please help set up a civil society umbrella group for Kailahun.' As a result they do not have a strong voice, which made it difficult for security personnel to identify civil society partnerships.

The two-day meeting covered a wide range of issues and gave people the chance to express their views on security and directly interact with security personnel. As one participant said, 'this initiative is an eye-opener for us. I have the feeling that the frank discussions around how we perceive ourselves will go a long way to bridge the gap between them [security] and us [civil society].' It was agreed that there was dire need for civil society to coordinate as a forum which could nominate representation on the DISEC. Security personnel acknowledged the importance of improving communication to the public. As the ONS representative said, 'I think the issue of DISEC going to the radio to discuss issues on security that is of use to the public will be an issue to be discussed at the next DISEC meeting. I consider this to be crucial.'

As a response to recommendations, within a month of the meeting the Kailahun District Civil Society Organisations (KAIDCSO) was formed and one of its members nominated and accepted by the DISEC to represent civil society on the committee, with a directive to report relevant information back to KAIDCSO. In the ensuing year, KAIDCSO members and security personnel have collaborated on a number of events and information-gathering activities, both as part of CR's Strengthening Citizens' Security project and independently.

In May 2008, two months prior to district elections, in response to recommendations from a security sector–civil society meeting, KAIDCSO and security personnel organised a local village-to-village campaign against the use of violence in the election process. For communities, watching civilians and military personnel walking together echoing slogans of non-violence was a historic event in terms of boosting public relations for the security sector.

The relationships developing between security personnel and civil society in Kailahun have noticeably helped to 'demystify' security and create information resources that are mutually beneficial to civil society and the security sector.

A panel of DISEC and LPPB members choose a pertinent local security topic to discuss and time is allocated to live phone-ins when the public ask questions and respond to panellists. These community radio programmes have helped support DISEC and LPPB efforts to respond to public security concerns and share outcomes from meetings that might otherwise remain restricted to the meeting room.

Another positive example of a successful security sector-civil society relationship is the Bo Peace and Reconciliation Movement (BPRM).[23] In recent years the BPRM has worked to develop links with decentralised government structures, particularly the justice and security sectors, in order to augment collaboration between civil society and the security sector. After the police's family support unit (FSU)[24] programme was developed in 2000 to address gender-based violence in communities, the BPRM complemented this work by collaboratively reconciling domestic disputes and helping victims file police reports of sexual and violent crimes against women and children. This collaboration was supported by a series of CR-facilitated dialogue and discussion sessions in 2004, which clarified roles between the police and the BPRM's alternative dispute resolution mechanisms, emphasising the complementary nature of both roles.

This initial collaboration with the security sector has led to a greater involvement by the BPRM in recent years. As a rule, it will only participate as mediator in large chiefdom disputes if both conflicting communities and state authorities endorse its involvement. This brought the BPRM in contact with the ONS, and the relationship that has since developed is an important example of the benefits of security sector and civil society collaboration. The ONS and BPRM have cooperated on a number of regional security threat cases that were successfully resolved. As a result of its reconciliation work and collaboration with the security sector, the BPRM was elected to serve as the civil society representative on the Bo DISEC in 2008.

There is no doubt that these mechanisms and processes are welcome reforms. But experience shows that it will take time, and more importantly commitment by all stakeholders, to overcome the current challenges. A large portion of the public is still unaware of the new security paradigm and relations between the security sector and civil society are still limited. As a result, crucial lines of communication are too often broken or ineffective (Figure 1 on page 204), with the most common public complaint being that when civil society reports concern security personnel, there is no feedback from the security sector. This does little to appease tensions within communities. This mechanism also assumes that civil society organisations have an effective structure for disseminating information and the capacity to reach grassroots level, which is generally not the case.

The ONS also develops public contacts at the provincial level, using opportunities to educate people about security structures. Projects such as Strengthening Citizens' Security are making a valuable contribution to the reform process in terms of security sector/civilian relations. But it is clear that the reform process cannot be entirely successful or even sustainable if the challenges noted above are not specifically addressed. Decades of mistrust and failed structures are not easily replaced by what is still a relatively young reform process.

Figure 1

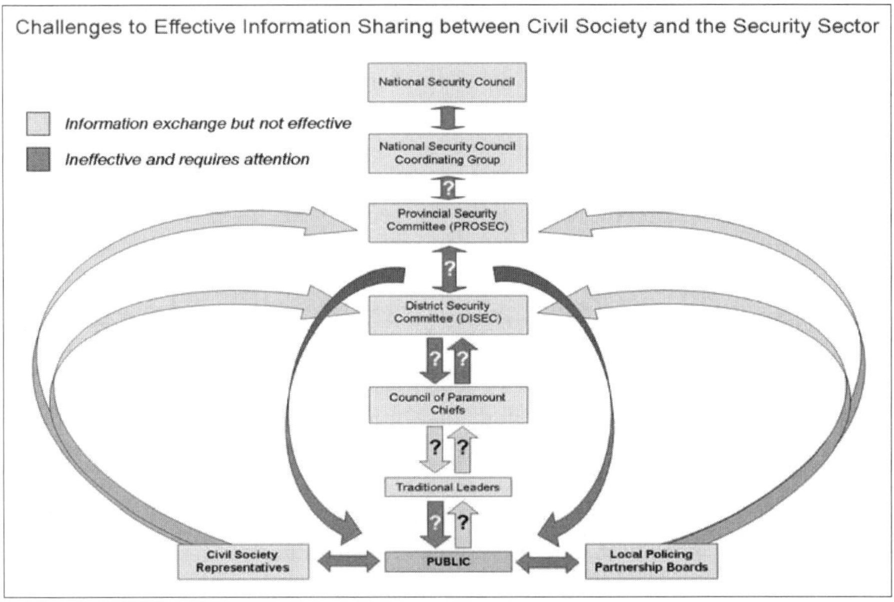

Reconciling Broken Relations Between the Military and Civilians

As stated earlier, the breakdown of public faith in the security sector reached its climax during the war. Restoring public trust and confidence in the armed forces is a long-term, high-priority process involving not only consolidation of the current peace but also healing of the suffering endured by civilians at the hands of the military.

Military reforms have been undertaken largely by the International Military Assistance Training Team (IMATT), funded by DFID and led by British military personnel. The UK government's long-term commitment to support IMATT in its 2002 memorandum of understanding with Sierra Leone initially helped alleviate public anxiety about a potential relapse into conflict. People viewed IMATT as a near-guarantee that the army would be unable to mutiny and training would raise the professional standards of the country's forces.

Today, Sierra Leoneans openly acknowledge that there have been visible changes in the professional performance of the renamed Republic of Sierra Leone Armed Forces over the last few years. The military has begun to recognise that community relationship-building is crucial to healing and is creating more opportunities to make positive contact with civilians. This commitment has extended to the military's budget, as each battalion receives limited funds for civil-military cooperation (CIMIC). For example, the CIMIC fund supports the coordination of sports activities in barracks with neighbouring communities. While this military involvement in communities is an important step towards improving local relations, like the police, the military would benefit from a nationwide public relations campaign to promote the 'new' reformed image.

During the first civil society–security sector meetings facilitated by CR in Kenema and Kailahun in 2006 as part of its Strengthening Citizens' Security project, there was a clear division between the military and civil society, based mainly on historic prejudice that manifested itself in an unwillingness to empathise with each other or understand positive changes that were taking place. Civil society pre-judged military personnel and assumed they had little interest in associating with the public. Women in particular, who were the target of brutal sexual violence during the war and remain subject to widespread gender-based violence, have understandably displayed deep distrust of the military. The military, too, pre-judged civil society as weak and disorganised.

Some of the project's activities supported civil-military interaction; there have been evident, albeit limited, improvements in how they relate to each other. In April 2008 CR collaborated with the Kailahun District Battalion to organise a football tournament between army officers and neighbouring communities (Box 2 on page 206). While this activity may appear basic, CR believes it is of enormous significance: it brought together former warring sides or former victims and perpetrators. It is one step in the right direction.

Box 2. Building relationships between the military and their neighbouring communities

In April 2008, CR collaborated with the Kailahun Battalion to organise a football tournament between army officers and neighbouring communities as part of the armed forces' Civil Military Cooperation (CIMIC) activities. Among the various teams was the Bike Renters Association (BRA), a self-organised commercial motorbike rental service formed in Bo district in 2003 as a response to the high level of unemployed ex-combatants. The BRA includes ex-combatants from the Civil Defence Force (CDF) and Revolutionary United Front (RUF) rebel movement who fought on opposing sides during the war.

The BRA parked their motorbikes near the barracks and sat side-by-side with military officers, drinking soft drinks and discussing football tactics. Competing on the football field were reformed ex-combatants from the three warring factions.

The tournament was open to the public; people from neighbouring communities came to cheer their teams and enjoy a free football match. The military were defeated by the BRA team and other teams and eventually lost the tournament. However, they took their defeat in good spirit and focused on the value of the event, which was to build civil society–security sector understanding and trust. At the end of each game, teams shook hands and shared a post-game social time, putting divides.

The 'Force for Good' – Sierra Leone Police

Reforming the security sector included promoting a new face to the public, one which would portray a sector working for and with the people. As the new security framework placed the onus of internal security on the Sierra Leone Police (SLP), images of a new, restructured, more professional police force were displayed around the country, with the slogan 'a force for good'. As part of the reform process, the SLP has made visible attempts to transform its image through its media and community relations departments. The use of high-ranking police officials, such as Assistant Inspector General Kadi Fakondo, to promote the reformed police service has contributed to elevating the image of police professionalism, particularly among women.

The creation of nationwide LPPBs has also increased collaboration between the SLP and civilians. Given the imbalance of the number of police in relation to the fast-growing population, police officials supported this measure in order to involve citizens in crime prevention. LPPBs embody the language of the 2005 security sector review: 'to encourage people to participate actively in their own security, additional support must be provided to the SLP to strengthen their public participation strategy through Local Policing Partnership Boards'.

In every district, LPPBs are non-partisan, inter-religious groups that work to create a peaceful and healthy police/community rapport. Their main responsibilities are to monitor police performance, act as a general forum for discussion and consultation on matters affecting policing and enhance public-police cooperation on crime prevention. As a result, LPPBs should perform a key role in ensuring that police enjoy the support of all sections of the community.

But the process has not been without its challenges. Civil society representatives are nominated by their community to serve on LPPBs, but neither police nor civil society has defined criteria for their selection. In addition, there is no effective induction programme to inform new representatives about their role. As one young man nominated to sit on a LPPB stated:

> I was nominated or asked to serve as a member of the partnership board. But since I was nominated, nobody has taught me what this is all about. I will appreciate it very much if you can ask them to explain what this is all about.

Establishment of FSUs has also been a welcome development within the SLP. Set up by the government in 2000, FSUs address gender-based violence and offer a venue, especially for women, to report domestic violence and sexual abuse cases. FSU offices are now located at police stations around the country. While it has been reported that FSUs lack basic infrastructure and communications support, they are playing an increasingly important role in the investigation of violence against women and children.

As with security structures in general, financial constraints are the greatest challenge to mainstreaming community policing. LPPBs do not have budgets; their work consists of police and members of the community meeting to discuss and share information about security concerns. It was clear during the Strengthening Citizens' Security project that in many rural districts, like Kenema and Kailahun, vast areas without viable roads make it extremely difficult for all members to meet. Aside from being severely understaffed, rural police stations lack vehicles and funds to fuel them to offer support to LPPBs or even adequately investigate cases. Without adequate resources, positive structures like LPPBs and FSUs run the risk of becoming dysfunctional and ineffective.

Youth and Security

In our work we have found one of the greatest challenges has been the dynamics between youth and the SSR process. Young people played a central role in Sierra Leone's conflict, as both fighters and victims of atrocities. After the war ended in 2002, around 70,000 ex-combatants went through a DDR programme. While DDR in Sierra Leone is officially considered as having substantially increased the country's immediate security, it has not adequately addressed the plight of marginalised young people. Six years on, many have not been successfully reintegrated into their communities and remain deprived of education, access to basic services and economic opportunities. Engaging and reintegrating war-affected youth are vital nation-building tasks and a security issue.

CR has always believed that youth can and should play a crucial role in rebuilding safer communities and contributing to the political, social and economic development of the country. One key step in this process is to ensure that young people and the security forces see each other as partners, able to share experiences and articulate common goals. This has already begun to happen.

Young people in Kailahun and Kenema got involved in campaigning for violence-free presidential elections in 2007, with the support of CR, security sector personnel and civil society organisations. As part of the Strengthening Citizens' Security project, CR brought together 29 students from Fourah Bay College, Njala University and Milton Margai College and civil society organisations to participate in an innovative academic study of concepts and dimensions of security from both practical and theoretical standpoints. Consideration of the country's SSR process was part of the course curriculum.

While there have been positive examples of collaboration, youth marginalisation and unemployment are severe. In December 2007 the government of Sierra Leone and the UN Peacebuilding Commission adopted the Sierra Leone peacebuilding cooperation framework. The framework identifies youth marginalisation and unemployment as a major challenge to the country's stability. It reminds us that the marginalisation and political exclusion of youth were identified by the Truth and Reconciliation Commission as one of the root causes of the civil war, and that today two-thirds of the country's youth are unemployed or under-employed. It is vital that SSR is accompanied by a national youth policy that delivers long-term, meaningful employment and empowerment opportunities. In the country's journey to stability, this could be the difference between peace and a relapse into violence.

Conclusion

There has been marked improvement, particularly since 2005, in the way the security sector engages with the public. Citizens generally have a more positive perception of security forces and institutions. In communicating with civil society, ONS officials speak of 'human security' and a 'holistic approach to security' – concepts that have helped formulate the 'security is everyone's business' motto. More than ever before, SSR offers opportunities for civil society participation at a local level in community policing, sharing information on potential and actual security threats, aspects of local decision making and trust building with the military through joint social activities.

One of the most recent and clearest indications of the positive impact of SSR in the eyes of civil society was the widespread public praise of the professionalism of security sector forces in the 2007 presidential elections. Given the historical background to this election and the potential for conflict, public tensions beforehand were high. Reassurances from the police that they had planned for all eventualities and the situation would be under control were met initially with great scepticism. While a number of local-level conflicts occurred in the run-up to voting (largely instigated by political party supporters), the SLP was able to address each incident and establish calm. Operating under more open public communications policies, the SLP was also able to communicate its mobilisation plans more widely; there was a corresponding increase in public trust. On election day, successful cooperation between the police and military was proof of a new era for security in Sierra Leone. The fact that there were no major disruptions to people's ability to vote increased public pride in their security forces.

CR's experience suggests that, despite poor access, integration of civil society in SSR has been more successful in rural districts. By focusing on the local context, solutions to problems and potential conflicts have been reached through collaboration between civil society and the security sector. While it has been possible to engage high-level, Freetown-based security sector representatives in the Strengthening Citizens' Security project, broader public engagement with the security sector in the urban Western Area, which includes Freetown, has been less visible. Entry points for security sector-civil society exchange in these areas remain more complex and challenging. The large number of civil society organisations in the

Western Area and the fragmented nature of these organisations make it difficult to identify genuine representation. While this state of affairs may justify the security sector's perception that civil society is not serious about participating in SSR, the sector itself does not yet have the capacity to reach out to large urban areas.

SSR in Sierra Leone has been lauded as a success; it has proved to be one of the most successful internal processes of reform since the end of the war. No doubt the significant financial and advisory UK government support and the commitment of the government have been factors in that success. But such success to date should not indicate that the reform process is concluded, or even sustainable. The real proof is yet to come, as donor support dwindles and the Sierra Leonean government has to make choices amid all the other economic and social challenges that the country still faces. Civil society will, no doubt, continue to play a critical role in this process.

Notes

1 Caparini, Marina (2004) 'The relevance of civil society response to security sector reform in developing and transitional countries', in Clem Mcartney, Martina Fischer and Oliver Wils (eds) *Security Sector Reform: Potentials and Challenges for Conflict Transformation,* Berghoff Handbook Dialogue Series.

2 UN Security Council (2007) 'Report of the Secretary General on Cross-border Issues in West Africa', UN Doc. S/2007/143, 13 March.

3 Ibid., p. 3.

4 Yasutomi, Atsushi and Carmans, Jan (2007) *Building Local Ownership in Security Sector Reform*, Leuven: Centre for Peace Research and Strategic Studies.

5 Ball, N., Biesheuval, P. and Olanisakin, F. (2007) 'Security and justice sector reform programming in Africa', DFID Evaluation Working Paper 23, London.

6 The review will be discussed below.

7 Gbla, Osman (2007) 'Security sector reform in Sierra Leone', in Len le Roux and Yemane Kidane (eds) *Challenges to Security Sector Reform in the Horn of Africa*, Pretoria: Institute for Security Studies.

8 Lord, David (ed.) (2000) *Paying the Price – The Sierra Leone Peace Process*, Conciliation Resources.

9 Inspiring the term 'sobels', a contraction of soldiers and rebels.

10 Lord, note 8 above.

11 For more details about civil society initiatives in the Sierra Leonean peace process see Lord, ibid.

12 Ball, Nicole, Brzoska, Michael, Kingman, Kees and Wulf, Herbert (2002) 'Accountability in the security sector', Bonn International Centre for Conversion report prepared for Human Development Report Office; Anderlini, Sanam Naraghi and Conaway, Camille Pampell (2004) 'Security sector reform', in *Inclusive Security, Sustainable Peace: A Toolkit for Advocacy and Action*, International Alert/Women Waging Peace.

13 The Campaign for Good Governance is an NGO formally established in July 1996 after Sierra Leone's first multi-party democratic elections in three decades. It promotes the building of democratic institutions, transparency and accountability in government, active citizen participation in the political process, voter education, human rights and the rule of law.

14 The Civil Defence Force was a paramilitary organisation that supported the elected government of Ahmed Tejan Kabbah against the rebel groups RUF and AFRC (Armed Forces Revolutionary Council) during the war.

15 International Crisis Group (2003) 'Sierra Leone: The state of security and governance', Africa Report 67, 2 September; Fayemi, J. 'Kayode, *Responsibility to Rebuild: Challenges of Security Sector Reform in Sierra Leone and Liberia.*

16 International Crisis Group, ibid.

17 The ONS was created in 2002 by the National Intelligence Act. It supports the National Security Council (NSC), the highest body in Sierra Leone's security structure, which is headed by the president and responsible for defining and implementing national security policy. The ONS is a non-political structure that serves as the NSC secretariat and coordinates security matters and policy initiatives. It collects ands analyses intelligence from all security agencies and provides the government with balanced intelligence assessments upon which to base policy decisions. The NSC also receives advice from the National Security Council Coordinating Group, which includes members of the Sierra Leone Police, the Republic of Sierra Leone Armed Forces, the Ministry of Defence, security agencies and the UN Observer Mission UN Integrated Office in Sierra Leone (UNIOSIL). The Central Intelligence and Security Unit is responsible for the collection of classified intelligence within and outside Sierra Leone. Also part of the country's security decision-making structure are the Joint Intelligence Committee (JIC), the provincial security committees (PROSECs – North, South, East and West) and the district security committees (DISECs). The JIC translates certain policy decisions of the NSC into formal intelligence requirements for the intelligence and security services. Both PROSECs and DISECs provide early warning to the government, via the ONS, of the existence or likelihood of any security threat. The DISECs meet more regularly than the PROSECs, and forward their security reports to the ONS through the latter.

18 The lingua franca of Sierra Leone.

19 Malan, Mark (2006) 'Post-conflict peacebuilding and national 'ownership' – Lessons from the Sierra Leone peace process', Seite 2, KAIPTC/ZIF, Berlin, February.

20 Jaye, Thomas and Gbla, Osman (2008) 'Parliamentary needs assessment: Parliamentary Oversight Committee on Defence, Internal and Presidential Affairs of the Republic of Sierra Leone'.

21 Ibid.

22 Local policing partnership boards are discussed later in this chapter.

23 In 1996 CR facilitated the development of the Bo Peace and Reconciliation Movement (BPRM) at a time when Sierra Leone was in dire need of peace intermediaries at the community level. The BPRM is a community-based voluntary peacebuilding organisation made up of a union of nine civil society groups, including regional ex-combatants, traders and teachers unions. Initially the BPRM was involved in engaging with RUF combatants to promote their demobilisation and reintegration. Since then it has trained over 350 community 'peace monitors' to facilitate conflict resolution processes within their chiefdoms, and is recognised at the national level for having helped resolve over a thousand cases of both armed violence and community dispute in the southern provinces.

The BPRM's success in reconciling disputes at local level has resulted in the movement being asked to intervene in conflicts around the country.

24 These are described in greater detail below.

Part IV

Conclusion

Chapter 13

Conclusions, Issues and Themes from the Sierra Leone Security Sector Transformation Process

Paul Jackson and Peter Albrecht

Introduction

As stated in the introductory chapter, in 2007 Sierra Leone conducted a general election without violence for the first time since the start of its conflict in the early 1990s. In the context of the horrendous levels of violence experienced by the people of Sierra Leone, this was a watershed event. While poverty levels in the country today are still significant and the country's institutional reforms are only in the nascent stage, there can be no doubt that most Sierra Leoneans are far better off in 2008 than they were in the late 1990s. This sense that the country is more secure and thus more capable of conducting democratic processes such as a peaceful election is due in large part to the palpable sense of *personal* security that Sierra Leoneans feel today.

What happened in Sierra Leone from the late 1990s until 2007 can only be described as a transformation. In the late 1990s it was a depleted, exhausted and ravaged country; by 2007 it was a country capable of presenting a democratic model to its people in the form of an election based on the simple standards of fairness, open debate and citizens exercising their right to vote. This transformation would not have been possible without the intervention of the international community, particularly the United Nations and the UK, and the leadership provided by a core of remarkable Sierra Leonean government officials. Both national and international leaders instituted, guided and managed system-wide reforms and tackled huge problems of reform over a long period of time and often in difficult circumstances.

This volume has provided a snapshot of views from within the process, and has been designed to provide a voice for those who are frequently not seen by external analysts looking at SSR. Instead of a polished set of analyses, they provide a picture of what those directly involved in the process actually think. The genesis of this volume was probably within one of the many workshops, seminars and meetings held in the UK and Sierra Leone over the time of this research and before. One of the noticeable elements of the process was that, while there may have been some coherence over time, not all parties agreed to some specific actions within that process. An aspect we tried to get at was the difference in perceptions of the process between the Sierra Leone team and the UK advisers who came and went. In fact, the chapters show that there was a common direction of travel but it was the Sierra Leonean team who really kept that all flowing, since the UK team was constantly changing.

This volume has not tried to provide comprehensive conclusions or even to draw a very clear picture, but rather it has attempted to shed light on some of the internal workings of the process of SSR within the country and provide a voice to those who were involved in different aspects of it. Agree or disagree, these voices are those from within the team carrying out the work, and so they have their own relevance and power. To anyone undertaking SSR this is the type of discourse that can be expected.

In spite of its reach, this volume discusses only a few of the salient conclusions and issues of the 1997–2007 Sierra Leone security system transformation process. We have outlined briefly the history of how this transformation developed in Sierra Leone and the context within which initial international intervention took place. We have provided a series of 11 chapters written by different people engaged in separate but connected activities within the overall transformation process. This final chapter attempts to draw together some of those aspects of the reform and sketch emerging themes from the history of the Sierra Leone transformation.

The Importance of Context and this Research

The history of the spiralling decline of the security situation in Sierra Leone is critical to the overarching context of what has been achieved through transformation of the country's security system. A spiral that started in the 1960s and reached its nadir in 1997 cannot be reversed by a three- or five-year development programme. This is at the heart of the reforms that eventually produced security system transformation in Sierra Leone. The pattern of international assistance that developed was one of fire-fighting at first, moving to increasingly medium-term programmes within an overall framework of long-term commitment to Sierra Leone.

It is important to point out that the research within this programme is heavily contextualised. It deals with the specific set of circumstances in Sierra Leone and conflicts that existed at that time. As such, any policy recommendations taken out of this experience need to be viewed with caution. In the case of Sierra Leone, for example, virtually all the infrastructure, including buildings and records, had been either destroyed or overrun by the RUF. UNAMSIL and the UK were in a position to support the GoSL in establishing basic security across the country. However, those charged with rebuilding the country were faced with a situation where basic security institutions had effectively ceased to function. In the area of intelligence, for example, international and Sierra Leonean officials literally sat around a meeting table and designed an entire intelligence system from scratch. This type of very basic reconstruction of institutions was not limited to intelligence; it was repeated across several other security institutions, including the Ministry of Defence (MoD). This level of starting with a blank sheet of paper is very rare in post-conflict or development environments, and may explain why, in the particular case of Sierra Leone's security system, non-state actors such as paramount chiefs were involved to only a limited degree, e.g. in the provincial and district security committees (PROSECs and DISECs) and the local partnership policing boards (LPPBs).

Specifically, although the creation of any governance system is ultimately political, the fact that several of the government's administrative functions had ceased to exist or been severely weakened meant that there was relatively less friction and resistance within the civil service than there could have been. Resistance occurred, of course, but it was relatively minor, because there were so few civil servants left. This is not meant to belittle the reconstruction efforts, but it does mean that the Sierra Leone experience may be very different from similar programmes in other countries and careful attention should be paid to policy transfer carried out in widely different contexts.

While the immediate security threat of the RUF had largely dissipated by 2000, the country was faced with a number of additional security issues. These included unstable borders and neighbours, the lack of a security infrastructure and discredited security institutions. In addition, the war had produced a rapidly urbanised population with no immediate prospects for improved economic status – a population that was about to be increased markedly by large numbers of ex-combatants who had been involved in extreme violence during Sierra Leone's conflict.

Fortunately, at the government level there was a very powerful consensus for reform and reconstruction among political figures, senior operational leaders and the external community. The commitment of a core team of Sierra Leonean leaders at political and senior civil service levels was absolutely critical in driving the reform process and exercising national ownership. Indeed, while international advisers, programme managers and officers came in for short periods of time, it was the Sierra Leoneans themselves who effected positive change.

The role of the external community in Sierra Leone is noteworthy in that the UK provided clear leadership. As the dominant donor by a considerable margin, the UK exhibited a remarkable lack of many external harmonisation issues that have occurred in other post-conflict contexts. This leadership, backed up by UK military involvement, proved critical in establishing credibility not only with the Sierra Leonean population and government, but also with the international community.

Key Issues and Themes emerging from Sierra Leone

There are, of course, several issues that arise within interventions that take place over long periods of time. In terms of Sierra Leone, there are a number of core themes that recur over time and have importance for the development of both Sierra Leone itself and SSR more generally. This list does not claim to be exhaustive, but represents some of the conclusions drawn from the research undertaken for the project on security system transformation in Sierra Leone, 1997–2007.

The importance of national ownership and engagement

One of the core lessons from Sierra Leone is that national ownership can become critical from a series of viewpoints, but this issue may not be straightforward.

First, it is impossible to overestimate the importance of finding capable people at both national and international levels. National ownership requires some confidence on the part of external actors, but also a degree of control on behalf of national owners. In Sierra Leone there has been a core group of individuals who have exercised collective ownership of the transformation process, even when they have had internal disagreements. Most importantly, on both international and national sides there has been a critical mass of good people who have managed to keep the process going under extremely trying circumstances.

At the political level there has been powerful and consistent buy-in to the overarching principle of security system transformation by the president and senior civil servants. This leadership has been important not only in terms of its ability to accept occasional intervention by international partners, but also in terms of developing a professional environment and garnering public support for the security system. Critically, there has also been a pool of operations personnel at senior ranks of the army, intelligence and police who have managed the process very effectively (including interface with external advisers) throughout the whole time period covered by this project, 1997–2007.

Secondly, the overall direction of the process has been driven by consistency within the core group of Sierra Leonean actors. Whereas international staff changed frequently (IMATT commanders in particular), many key Sierra Leonean staff engaged in the process remained remarkably consistent. While the role of international advisers cannot be overestimated, it is incorrect simply to conclude that the transformation process was 'externally driven'. It is Sierra Leoneans, not external actors, who have invested almost a decade – or longer – in the process of transforming the security system, and with it the country as a whole. This continuity over a significant period of time has meant that a number of the key drivers of the process remained in place and provided both policy and operational consistency.

Sierra Leonean continuity and oversight

This continuity of Sierra Leonean staff, holders of valuable institutional memory, has also enabled the GoSL to manage external donor relationships coherently and increased trust between UK and Sierra Leonean actors. The smooth-working UK-Sierra Leone relationship was also aided by the UK's consistent support and the absence of other significant donors.

Of course, there is a danger in this particular approach, in that a small group of powerful individuals can have the political and financial clout to see their decisions implemented while hijacking the process and preventing other input. This is a particular concern in a young democracy with few consolidated checks and balances. While this is a point well taken, our rejoinder to it relative to Sierra Leone is 'what other choice is/was there?'.

The development of civil society as an effective oversight mechanism in Sierra Leone has been driven in part by some of the institutions encompassed by the security system. In particular, the ONS and SLP have been instrumental in engaging civil society through institutions like the

PROSECs, DISECs and LPPBs, but the Republic of Sierra Leone Armed Forces has also sought to engage citizens by improving public perceptions of the army. The results from the survey produced in support of this project indicate clearly that these efforts have had a positive impact. Generally speaking, Sierra Leoneans no longer feel threatened by the army or the SLP, whereas before the onset of the transformation process, indeed before the conflict, they certainly did. This change in popular perception, while not conclusive, indicates that the engagement with civil society has had at least some success. It is worth pointing out here, however, that only in 2006 was a structured attempt made to engage civil society as part of the programming in support of the country's security system transformation process. Civil society's security system oversight role is still in the nascent stage.

By far the least developed element of oversight within the system is at the political, including parliamentary, level. Due to issues within and between ministries and ministers and the lack of functioning parliamentary structures, one of the key oversight mechanisms within the government is the ONS. The question remains, however: who monitors the ONS? In the longer term, the issue of ONS oversight may become politically risky; without proper parliamentary oversight and UK support, the security system may be hindered from developing into a truly democratically led set of institutions.

UK coordination

It is difficult to overestimate the importance of the individual international adviser who makes virtually all initial moves in coordinating external support with the host government.

Of course, the impact of one personality on any process is driven in part by the importance of individuals *per se*. However, in the Sierra Leonean security transformation context it has also been a function of the lack of a coherent UK government strategy, which drove a series of disagreements on the ground among MoD, Foreign and Commonwealth Office (FCO) and DFID officials. This was not helped by the lack of a DFID country office in Sierra Leone until 2005. Thus DFID decision-making power reflected a wider set of coordination difficulties at the UK government level. These difficulties still exist today, despite the development of joint pooling mechanisms between departments, including the Global Conflict Prevention Pool. Given these challenges, in some ways the level of coherence reached within Sierra Leone is surprisingly good, due in large part due to the crucial role played by individuals.

However, since Sierra Leone lacked virtually all of the basic tools and infrastructure necessary to govern and speed was of the essence, it was particularly important to get *something* up and functioning rather than leave a power vacuum. DFID found itself with no time to conduct formal planning procedures that would have held intervention up for a significant time.

In the event, DFID fell back on its professional experience in dealing with these types of situations and placed experienced staff from within and outside DFID in the field to assess and act on needs. These were not people who were necessarily well versed in formal project management; they were *operations professionals* experienced in running projects on the ground rather than experts in developing logical frameworks. This was a critical skill-set in a situation where there was no way that the UK government could have access to all of the relevant information fast enough. Thus security-related programming in Sierra Leone became a response to immediate needs.

Sierra Leonean exceptionalism

Another significant aspect of UK collaboration with the GoSL was the signing of a memorandum of understanding (MoU) in 2002, a long-term agreement between the two countries scheduled to last until 2012. Because UK engagement was primarily the result of a coalition of high-level British politicians who were committed to a country they felt could not be allowed to fall further into chaos, there was strong pressure on UK ministries to work together on Sierra Leone. When one takes into consideration the general difficulties of cross-department collaboration, this unusual level of UK coordination of efforts is an achievement in and of itself.

By extension, the experience of Sierra Leone influenced the creation of the conflict pool approach to managing aid funding, aimed at enforcing shared strategies across the FCO, MoD and DFID. However, there have been a number of internal issues regarding the management of these pools, not least of which has been the rapid and constant change of personnel involved with decision-making on funding priorities. This sometimes dizzying change of UK actors has led at times to a lack of long-term coherence. Because of changing UK priorities and staff inexperience regarding funding decisions, there have been times when the future of security-related programming in Sierra Leone has been in question.

Despite these difficulties, the early UK-Sierra Leone commitment to work together and the development of an overarching framework encompassed by the MoU were critical in establishing trust between the two parties. This was certainly the main driver in developing the increased confidence in the future of a GoSL backed by the UK, and allowed UK expatriate staff to play a role as external catalysts in change and guarantors of trust in the government. In turn, the relationship of trust between the UK and Sierra Leone helped develop and nurture a credible group of Sierra Leonean staff as effective counterparts.

Sustainability

One of the issues in discussing sustainability in the context of Sierra Leone is what exactly we mean by the term. A purist definition dictates that a government should be able to sustain its own security institutions without external interference. However, strict adherence to this definition would preclude *any* functioning security apparatus in sub-Saharan Africa. The key word here is ‘functioning’, and it is on the relevant functions that are expected of Sierra Leone’s security system that we need to concentrate.

Dysfunctional security institutions are prevalent in many parts of the world and are particularly prone to direct involvement in politics. In the long term, external military involvement in states where security institutions have ceased to function (except in a political sense) may be far more expensive and less ‘sustainable’ than providing steady long-term support and guidance to security institutions with the aim of preventing their becoming dysfunctional in the first place. Small amounts of investment over a longer period of time may produce a more functional and sustainable security system than no investment, steady decline and then the inevitable crisis followed by the inevitable intervention.

There are, of course, specific operational issues about the relative sizes of armies, police and intelligence systems that need to be addressed. In particular, the experience in Sierra Leone of linking the production of a security sector review where threats are identified to transforming the security system to counter these threats can be developed elsewhere. There are a few weaknesses in this approach, particularly the risk of ignoring external regional and international linkages. (For example, the RUF did not exist in Sierra Leone alone, but also in Guinea and Liberia.) Regional dimensions of the conflict and of any potential future conflict imply that a national security strategy should incorporate significant links with regional partners to prevent any future uprisings falling between ‘national cracks’ relating to boundaries and jurisdictions.

The issue of sustainability also leads to a clash between external actors and national owners of the process. It is inevitable that there will be differences in perceptions of what is or is not sustainable in the long run, as well as what operational capability is required or feasible. Like much of SSR – and development activities more broadly – this is due in part to questions of political balance and pragmatism and, at some level, of balancing realistic strategic planning with plans that amount to wish lists. There may be hard decisions to be made about the form and function of defence and policing infrastructures, vehicles and equipment that will need strong leadership at the top. However, there must also be commitment from external donors to retrain and reconfigure security institutions that are fit for purpose, as opposed to mirrors of security systems in the donor country.

How does the Sierra Leonean Experience Affect Perceptions of SSR?

While many activities are now implemented in the name of SSR, the concept remains rather weak, not only in Sierra Leone but also within the UK government. Given the length of time that the UK has been involved in security system transformation in Sierra Leone and how often this experience is used as an example of how to do SSR internationally, this is in itself a concern that needs to be addressed.

As we have seen, a number of different factors led to development of the security system in Sierra Leone, not least the fact that at the beginning of UK involvement there was no strategy or blueprint of what this process would entail. In effect, the SSR policy that exists within the UK government is in many ways a *post hoc* rationalisation of a diverse set of activities that clustered well within Sierra Leone. However, in order to back that conclusion up, we need to unravel this issue even further.

The specific experience of people on the ground who are able to react to situation and context is very different to having a coherent plan of SSR. Clearly SSR has taken place in Sierra Leone, but it has done so largely without a framework within which to act. The critical factors appear to have been the existence of a strong group of national owners who have remained relatively constant over time and a key group of external advisers who were able to work together to support the Sierra Leonean group. Even though the individuals themselves have not been constant, the constant presence of external groups which managed to work together (the UN, World Bank and DFID) and specific support mechanisms (IMATT in particular, as well as individuals supporting key security institutions like the ONS and CISU) has been critical in ensuring a constant upward curve of post-conflict reconstruction. In many ways, the experience of Sierra Leone shows how dedicated people can, over time, achieve an awful lot.

Current debates on SSR emphasise holistic and integrated approaches to the reform of institutions that deliver internal and external security. These debates consider the institutions of security, intelligence, governance and justice. At the same time, there are serious tensions concerning the further development of SSR when normal planning functions of government departments come into play. The question that Sierra Leone asks today is how far can one actually plan a series of policies that are based in part on activities on the ground in response to immediate needs, activities that are, by definition, in a constant state of flux?

This question, in turn, raises a number of questions about SSR programming in general and how far SSR can indeed be programmed into the future. While there is a clear set of activities and principles within SSR, this does not amount to a plan *per se*. These principles and activities are more like a series of guidelines or a 'direction of travel'. While this may be an important issue in itself, it does not lend itself to development planning in the sense of neat three-year project cycles. The experience of Sierra Leone, where transformation rather than reform was taking place, shows that SSR is governed by context and entry points and is, above all, an evolutionary process guided by individuals. This emphasises the importance of well-qualified and experienced individuals on the ground empowered to take decisions and build relationships based on trust.

Conclusion: Was It All Worth It?

Sierra Leone remains near the bottom of the league in terms of human development. However, it is clear that there have been significant gains in terms of basic living conditions for the majority of the population. In particular, the pattern of security threats faced by most people has changed markedly from an assumed threat from security forces themselves to more 'conventional' forms of threat, including domestic violence, street crime (frequently violent), smuggling (particularly of drugs), human trafficking and youth unemployment.

The survey conducted as part of this study covered just a small sample of districts across the country, but trends towards improved perceptions of security and security threats in all areas – urban and rural – are positive. These patterns in themselves, however, have significant implications. The demand for particular types of security has changed; this needs to be reflected in security provision across the country, notably changing protection from extreme violence to a more recognisable set of concerns based around criminal activity.

Study results indicated that improved civil-military relations and professionalism of security actors produced by the transformation process are being maintained. Respondents expressed the feeling that civil-military dialogue had increased and they feel less threatened today by security actors such as soldiers and police. The concern about youth unemployment is reflected in a number of papers on post-war Sierra Leone that point to the potential threat of alienation of groups that identify themselves with those who originally took to the bush under the auspices of the RUF.

The threat of returning to some form of violent conflict remains, particularly in the countryside. In urban areas, public concern about street crime underscores the need to address the issue of youth unemployment. Like many countries, Sierra Leone is experiencing the issue of unemployed young men becoming the foot-soldiers of criminal gangs and increasing the incidence of street crime.

The growth of criminal activity and persistence of unemployment and social exclusion also point to a continuing need for an effective SLP presence in the countryside. At the same time, the existence of gangs engaged in the smuggling of drugs and people, for instance, means that the SLP and other security agencies need to continue to improve their own capabilities and develop cross-border links. For example, a recent dramatic increase in drug activity in neighbouring Guinea indicates that SLP linkages with its cross-border counterparts should become a priority. All of these current security challenges point to the need to change and enhance the skill-sets employed by security services to reflect the changes in the threats faced.

Given the weakness of Sierra Leone following the war, the development of gangs happened relatively rapidly, and while security has improved, there is no way in which the total security system transformation process could be said to have been completed, even after ten years.

The importance of the justice sector emerged in most of the discussions we have had during our research. In particular, a number of security stakeholders expressed that woeful delays in processing and sentencing criminals by the justice system have a widespread negative impact on the morale of the SLP. Clearly, support for continued development of the SLP must be linked with simultaneous development of the criminal justice system, as is currently done through the Justice Sector Development Programme (JSDP).

At the same time, it is clear that for most people in Sierra Leone justice is local and involves a wide range of non-formal and semi-formal conflict resolution mechanisms, including village elders, religious figures and chiefs. However, reports from Kono, for example, suggest that some of these mechanisms as they are being applied result in controversial land allocations, an extremely sensitive issue that was one of the social causes of the war. One implication of the study's findings is that justice reforms should pay more attention to non-formal justice mechanisms, partly addressed through the ongoing JSDP, while at the same time encouraging an accessible SLP and magistrates' system. One of the issues that remains with 'traditional justice' is that traditionally some groups have been excluded from these processes.

Overall, it is clear that public perceptions of security in Sierra Leone have markedly improved and security system transformation has managed to enhance public knowledge of and confidence in the security services. The fact that more than 40 per cent of the survey's respondents understood the functions of local intelligence infrastructures is, in itself, a tremendous success. If the public continue to be informed about and involved with local security infrastructures, Sierra Leone has begun a civil-security sector relationship that could rival those in more developed countries.

Finally, public and stakeholder confidence in security and the success of the security system transformation process as a whole resulted in remarkably free and fair elections in 2007, which were conducted without significant violence or the political involvement of security services. An incumbent government left office and a new government took over, which is something that deserves to be applauded loudly in contemporary Africa.

List of Contributors

Peter ALBRECHT is a PhD researcher at the Danish Institute for International Studies (DIIS) and Copenhagen Business School, focusing on local level implementation of security sector reform (SSR) in Sierra Leone. Previously, he was Governance and Conflict Adviser in the UK's Stabilisation Unit and Senior Programme Officer in International Alert's Peacebuilding Issues Programme. He holds an MSc in Nationalism and Ethnicity from London School of Economics and Political Science (LSE) and an MA Research Degree in Anthropology and Ethnography from Aarhus University, Denmark.

Robert ASHINGTON-PICKETT was the Intelligence and Security Advisor to the Office of National Security (ONS) and the Central Intelligence and Security Unit (CISU) in Sierra Leone from 2000-2003. Robert has prior to and after this work held several positions in both the private and the public sector.

Kellie H. CONTEH heads the Office of National Security in Sierra Leone as the National Security Coordinator.

Kadi FAKONDO is Assistant Inspector General of Police, Training in the Sierra Leone Police.

Aldo S. GAETA is the Assistant Director in the Defence Fraud Analysis Unit in the British Ministry of Defence. He served as Civilian Adviser to the Sierra Leone Ministry of Defence from 2003-2006.

Rosalind HANSON-ALP is Country Programme Director for IBIS Liberia. She previously held the position of West Africa Programme Coordinator for Conciliation Resources, and was based in Freetown, Sierra Leone.

Anthony C. HOWLETT-BOLTON is currently Police and Justice Adviser to the Security and Justice Group in the UK's Stabilisation Unit and a lead adviser to DfID Sudan on policing. He was the Component Manager, Safety and Security, for the Justice Sector Development Programme (JSDP) from 2005-2007.

Paul JACKSON is Professor of African Politics at the University of Birmingham, UK. He is currently Head of the School of Government and Society at the University. Previously he was Director of the International Development Department and of the Global Facilitation Network for Security Sector Reform. He is a political economist who has worked on governance and security issues for a wide range of different organisations. He has worked in many different environments including several African countries, Nepal, India, Bangladesh, Georgia, Romania and China, and first went to Sierra Leone just after the war in 2002 where he worked on decentralisation and governance. He has been a frequent visitor since then.

Al-Hassan KHARAMOH KONDEH is currently the Director of Administration, Finance and Consular Affairs in the Sierra Leone Ministry of Foreign Affairs and International Co-operation. Prior to this, he worked in the SLMoD in different capacities, including Director of Policy. He holds a Master of Science degree in Governance and Development Management from the University of Birmingham and a postgraduate Diploma in Public Administration from the Institute of Public Administration and Management (USL).

Barry LE GRYS is a serving Brigadier in the UK Armed Forces. He is a Royal Engineer by cap badge and is currently focused upon generating military engineers with the right equipment, procedures and training for operations worldwide, Afghanistan in particular. He is also the Land Force proponent for Military Assistance to Civil Effect including sponsorship of the Military Stabilization Support Group (concentrating upon support to the Provincial Reconstruction Team in Helmand Province, Afghanistan). He served with the UN Assistance Mission in Sierra Leone through 2001, responsible for military planning, and in 2005/6 he was the Military Advisor to the Government of Sierra Leone and commander of the International Military Advisory and Training Team (IMATT).

Alfred NELSON-WILLIAMS is Chief of Defence Staff, Republic of Sierra Leone Armed Forces. He has held various appointments, including Assistant Chief of Defence Staff Operations and Plans and Military Spokesman, Deputy Chief of Defence Staff and Chief of Defence Staff.

Emmanuel OSHO COCKER has over 38 years experience in public administration and public sector management, starting as an Assistant Secretary in 1971 in the Civil Service of Sierra Leone and moving up the career ladder to serve in various prominent positions including Permanent Secretary in several ministries, Development Secretary, and Establishment Secretary. He was engaged by DFID on contract from 2001 to 2008 as Coordinator and later Director of Public Sector Reform working with the Government of Sierra Leone. He is presently Secretary to the President of the Republic of Sierra Leone.

Mark WHITE is the British Government's Regional Conflict Adviser for West Africa. Formerly, he was DfID's Security Sector Advisor, and before that, he spent two and a half years as the manager of DfID's Security Sector Reform and Justice Sector Development programmes in Sierra Leone.

About the Geneva Centre for the Democratic Control of Armed Forces (DCAF)

The Geneva Centre for the Democratic Control of Armed Forces (DCAF) is an international foundation whose mission is to assist the international community in pursuing good governance and reform of the security sector. To this end, the Centre develops and promotes appropriate norms at the international and national levels, determines good practices and relevant policy recommendations for effective governance of the security sector, and provides in-country advisory support and practical assistance programmes to all interested actors.

Detailed information is available at www.dcaf.ch

Geneva Centre for the Democratic Control of Armed Forces (DCAF)
Rue de Chantepoulet 11, PO Box 1360, CH-1211 Geneva 1, Switzerland
Tel: + 41 22 741 77 00; fax: + 41 22 741 77 05; e-mail: info@dcaf.ch

Geneva Centre for the Democratic Control of Armed Forces (DCAF)

Timothy Donais (Ed.)
Local Ownership and Security Sector Reform
The notion of "local ownership" has emerged in recent years as part of the contemporary commonsense of security sector reform (SSR). While the argument that externally driven reform processes are unsustainable is now widely accepted, the principle of local ownership has proven difficult to both define and operationalise. With contributions by leading practitioners, both "insiders" and "outsiders", *Local Ownership and Security Sector Reform* subjects the broader issue of local ownership to critical scrutiny, furthers the debate on what local ownership is and why it matters, and explores how ownership issues have played out in the context of specific SSR case studies.
2008, 312 S., 29,90 €, br., ISBN 978-3-8258-1652-0

LIT Verlag Berlin – Münster – Wien – Zürich – London
Auslieferung Deutschland / Österreich / Schweiz: siehe Impressumsseite

Hans Born; Albrecht Schnabel (Eds.)

Security Sector Reform in Challenging Environments

More often than not Security Sector Reform (SSR) takes place against many odds, in barely enabling political, security, economic and social environments. Such difficult contexts may be characterised by widespread corruption, ongoing violence, imprecise, open-ended or non-inclusive peace agreements and post-conflict architectures, lack of resources, ''stolen'' or impending elections or referenda – all circumstances that stand in the way of full-fledged, holistic and sustainable SSR efforts. Following an overview of ''ideal'' SSR requirements, contrasted with typical obstacles inhibiting SSR efforts, the main body of this volume offers evidence-based analyses of positive and negative SSR records in barely enabling environments, drawing on the experiences of specific national and international SSR programmes and experiences in Africa, the Americas, Asia and Europe. Lessons learned from these experiences are intended to feed into theoretical re-thinking of SSR policy frameworks as well as to help practitioners in designing and implementing effective and sustainable SSR in challenging environments.

, 2009, 288 pp., 29,90 €, br., ISBN-CH 978-3-643-80013-8

LIT Verlag Berlin – Münster – Wien – Zürich – London

Auslieferung Deutschland / Österreich / Schweiz: siehe Impressumsseite

Cornelius Friesendorf
The Military and Law Enforcement in Peace Operations
Lessons from Bosnia-Herzegovina and Kosovo
After war, police forces are often unable or unwilling to put pressure on suspected war criminals, organized crime groups, and other spoilers of sustainable peace. This book sheds light on the role of international military forces in post-conflict law enforcement. Drawing on numerous interviews, it shows that EU and NATO military forces have not systematically fought serious crime in Bosnia-Herzegovina and Kosovo. International actors need to better balance their own interests as well as the requirement to separate military and police functions with the urgent need to protect individuals in war-torn countries. The policy recommendations in the book are aimed at contributing to more effective, efficient, and legitimate peace operations in the Balkans and beyond.
, 2010, 208 pp., 29,90 €, br., ISBN-CH 978-3-643-80043-5

LIT Verlag Berlin – Münster – Wien – Zürich – London
Auslieferung Deutschland / Österreich / Schweiz: siehe Impressumsseite